RECLAIMING JUDAISM

as a
SPIRITUAL PRACTICE

HOLY DAYS
and SHABBAT

RABBI GOLDIE MILGRAM

JEWISH LIGHTS Publishing

Woodstock, Vermont

Reclaiming Judaism as a Spiritual Practice:
Holy Days and Shabbat

2004 First Printing
© 2004 by Goldie Milgram

Library of Congress Cataloging-in-Publication Data
Milgram, Goldie, 1955–
Reclaiming Judaism as a spiritual practice : holy days and Shabbat / Goldie Milgram.
  p. cm.
Includes bibliographical references and index.
ISBN 1-58023-205-1 (pbk.)
1. Fasts and feasts—Judaism. 2. Spiritual life—Judaism. I. Title.
BM690.M543 2004
296.4'3—dc22

2004011533

10 9 8 7 6 5 4 3 2 1

Manufactured in Canada
Cover Design: Sara Dismukes

Published by Jewish Lights Publishing
A Division of LongHill Partners, Inc.
Sunset Farm Offices, Route 4, P.O. Box 237
Woodstock, VT 05091
Tel: (802) 457-4000   Fax: (802) 457-4004
www.jewishlights.com

This book is dedicated
to the memory of my friend and mentor,
Louise P. Vanett,
and in honor of my teacher,
Rabbi Zalman Schachter-Shalomi.

CONTENTS

ACKNOWLEDGMENTS

This book has been made possible by a grant from the Nathan Cummings Foundation, with the support and encouragement of Dr. Ruth Durchslag.

Generous, creative, perceptive, honest, and direct, the *minyan* of my life is forever enriched by the companionship of the Reclaiming Judaism Trans-denominational Internet Focus Group: Adam Beitman, Reva Bernstein, Dr. Ivan Bub, Suzie Garfinkle-Chevrier, Gary Cohen, Esq., Ellen Weaver, Carola deVries Robles, Dr. Fred Harwin, Lynn Hazan, Iva Kaufman, Dr. Paul Levy, Gerrit Locher, Dr. Samuel Milgram, Karen Stuck Mortensen, Shira Reiss, Lara Rosenthal, Rabbi Robert Scheinberg, Nancy Sher, Cantor Meredith Stone, Dr. Sharon Ufberg, and Dr. Laura Vidmar.

The author's heartfelt appreciation goes to:

The core team of P'nai Yachadut—Reclaiming Judaism: Sara Harwin, Dr. Sharon Ufberg, and Rabbi Shohama Wiener. This is the teaching and educational research non-profit that is the predominant vehicle for my work in the world.

My dear hubbatzin, Barry Bub, who, during the course of this work's research and writing, drove to over forty-four sites of teaching and mutual exploration around the world. So often I sat beside you, silently working on my laptop and occasionally asking for help, which you offered with a generous spirit accompanied by many important insights.

Ann Edelstein, my literary agent, whose belief in the importance of this material and whose warmth, clarity, professionalism, and creativity sustained this process at every step.

Stuart M. Matlins, publisher of Jewish Lights, who has created a much-needed publishing vehicle of quality and integrity for this time when Judaism is being renewed in spirituality and meaning.

Dr. Ruth Durchslag, for so selflessly and unobtrusively providing the support for an entire season of my life's work.

Emily Wichland, Judy Kern, Lara Rosenthal, and Tracy Bernstein, four amazing copyeditors, who read and edited with talent and gave professional guidance with real feeling for the text.

The generous guidance and encouragement of a number of experienced authors gave me the courage to do this, particularly Rabbis David Cooper, Wayne Dosick, Nancy Fuchs-Kreimer, Michael Lerner, and Rami Shapiro, as well as Arthur Kurzweil, Marcia Cohen Spiegel, and Dr. Gene Gendlin.

The following teachers have been a primary source of inspiration to me. I hope readers will seek out these remarkable beings and their works: Rabbi Judith Abrams, Rabbi Samuel Barth, Dr. Judith Baskin, Sylvia Boorstein, Rabbi David Cooper, Rabbi Gail Diamond, Dr. Marcia Falk, Dr. Tikva Frymer-Kensky, Rabbi Yaacov Gabriel, Dr. Elliot

Ginsberg, Dr. David Golomb, Rabbi Lynn Gottlieb, Dr. Arthur Green, Rabbi Shefa Gold, Rabbis Victor and Nadia Gross, Dr. Judith Hauptman, Rabbi Linda Holtzman, Dr. Irving Greenberg, Dr. Aaron Katcher, Rabbi Myriam Klotz, Arthur Kurzweil, Dr. Shulamit Magnus, Rabbi Isaac Mann, Rabbi Itzchak Marmorstein, Dr. George McClain, Rabbi Leah Novick, Dr. Peter Pitzele, Dr. Judith Plaskow, Rabbi Marcia Prager, Rabbi Geelah Rayzl Raphael, Dr. Simcha Paull Raphael, Dr. Lester Ruiz, Rabbi Margot Stein, Rabbi Jeff Roth, Peninnah Schram, Rabbi Zalman Schachter-Shalomi, Hazzan Neil Schwartz, Rabbi Daniel Siegel, Rabbi Rami Shapiro, Dr. Dick Snyder, Dr. Jacob Staub, Dr. Adin Steinsaltz, Dr. David Teutsch, Rabbi Shawn Zevit, Dr. Arthur Waskow, Rabbi Shohama Wiener, Rabbi David Zaslow, and Dr. Aviva Zornberg.

I wish also to draw your attention to teachers who changed my life in a variety of ways, who are now *niftar*, departed from this world far too soon and far too young: Rabbis Seth Brody, Shlomo Carlbach, and David Wolfe-Blank, *z"l.*

And finally, deepest appreciation and abounding love to my students everywhere. Your questions and responses are the best teachers.

With love and appreciation from my heart to all of yours,
R'Goldie Milgram

INTRODUCTION

Religion has had a terrible history. Tens of millions of people have died of its side effects in Jerusalem, Belfast, the Crusades, the Salem Witch Trials, the Spanish Inquisition, and the World Trade Center. And let us not forget the Buddhist atrocities in Sri Lanka; the Hindu underpinnings of the caste system; the Bosnian Orthodox Christian ethnic cleansing of Muslim and Roman Catholic Croats; and the Muslim genocide of Catholics in East Timor, among many examples, including the ever-raging situation in the Middle East.

It is tempting to throw the baby out with the bathwater, to declare oneself a secular humanist and be done with religion. Religion is clearly a dangerous entity.

I almost did that—I almost walked away from being Jewish. Were you ever asked to make a list of oxymorons in high school? Mine included Jewish spirituality, women rabbis, and honest politicians. The Judaism I grew up with was desiccated, disappointing, depressing, and, quite frankly, boring. Stunned by my own experiences of anti-Semitism and frustrated by sexism, I surveyed other religious options but, in the end, still felt called to uncover the meaning of being born a Jew.

I embarked on a passionate search to find the missing puzzle pieces, to reclaim Judaism. Then, one day, after years of thoughtful input from seekers and teachers the world over, it all came together. I was able to see the elegant infrastructure of Judaism, as well as the missing ingredient: *applied spirituality*. In Hebrew school and rabbinical school we are taught the body of the tradition. On my spiritual journey, I've found those who understand how to restore its soul. The combination is exquisite.

Has your heart ever been broken—by divorce, loss, disappointment, awe, fear, hope? Have you multitasked, worked past the level of your endurance, accumulated possessions, jumped the hurdles, and gotten the grades only to wonder, "Is that all there is?" Do you wish for a life that is physically grounded, emotionally satisfying, intellectually expansive, and profoundly connected? These are the qualities Judaism can provide when you understand how to practice it.

A healthy religious system supports life by infusing it with meaning, integrity, and joy. It offers holy day practices and everyday practices, as it is written in Deuteronomy 6:7, "for when you walk on the way, when you lie down and when you rise up." Here, in *Reclaiming Judaism as a Spiritual Practice*, you will find a wide variety of Jewish practices, offered as a series of "recipes," that support, expand, and provide a meaningful context for the experience of being alive. "Taste" them as a way of enriching your own religious experience.

Suppose you have never tasted _haroset_, the Passover ritual food made of specific ground fruits, nuts, spices, and wine that symbolizes the building mortar used by the Israelites when they were slaves in Egypt. Since you will be building memories and meaning at every step of a _haroset_ experience, ideally you will be able to prepare it with a dear friend, an elder, a partner, or a child assisting you. In your heart you might have feelings about the holiness and wholeness of preparing sacred foods for a seder; by sharing these feelings as you labor, you build and convey to others important and unforgettable life nutrients.

At the actual Passover seder, as you taste the *haroset,* deepen your Passover practice by discussing its metaphorical meanings. For example, you might invite an elder to share her thoughts on the "building materials" that are important for a satisfying life. As others offer additional perspectives, the emphasis might shift to contemplation of which "building blocks" in life lead to the feeling of being enslaved and which build freedom? And even if you have solid blocks to set in place, what do you need as the mortar, the "glue" that holds a life together? The range of what can emerge through this kind of exchange is limitless and will vary according to the stages of life and the human condition of those at the table at any moment in history.

You won't truly experience *haroset,* and know whether it speaks to you or not, until you select a recipe, collect the ingredients, then actually prepare the *haroset,* taste the results, and savor the flavor and texture as its symbolic meaning comes alive at a seder that serves the inner circle of your life.

The same is true of all the spiritual practices in this book. You can't experience or judge them until you've tried them. No one expects to use every recipe in a cookbook. As you read, you might think about which ones sound good, which ones you'd like to try. This book is designed to be a lifelong resource you can turn to as holidays come around, so that you can test specific recipes in their season.

I hope you'll avoid analyzing the recipes before you've tried them, because the moment you begin to analyze spirituality, it's lost. After you've tasted and savored the flavors, however, you might reflect on the experience. If a practice seemed valuable, continue it. But if anything I suggest strikes you as unsafe or inappropriate, don't do it; trust yourself and your body. Your needs come first. There are no requirements here. This is not a cult. The Judaism you will be experiencing is an evolving tradition of which you are an empowered heir. That said, sometimes things that seem uncomfortable at first provide the greatest opportunities for growth and point to places where it is possible to go deeper with a good, safe teacher. My intention is to provide a wide enough variety to suit many appetites.

Before you begin to cook and taste, it may prove valuable to read this book cover to cover; take in the gestalt of Judaism, see how the practices fit together, notice the evolution of ideas, and enjoy the stories that illustrate what it is like to live this revitalized Judaism.

The synergy between practices tends to become quite profound. As an example, let's take the Shema, a verse from Deuteronomy found in the mezuzah, in *tefillin*, and in every daily and holiday service that teaches the unity of all being. It is the prayer for when you believe you are on the brink of certain death and feel your soul ready to cross the threshold to the next level of being. It is also a spiritual practice to say the Shema before going to sleep at night, which is like putting up a mezuzah on the threshold of your dreams to help you remember the importance of listening to the voices there, because they are also the voice of G*d.[1] I will do my best to reveal these kinds of synergies as we go along.

[1] I have chosen to represent the word *God* as G*d. This is to preserve the Jewish practice of approaching the Mysterious Evolving in which we are embedded with an attitude of humility, respect, and awe.

But what about faith? While a connection to G*d might be the by-product, you don't need the "G" word to experience the benefits of the practices taught here. A simple sense of awe in the face of our huge, fascinating, inspiring, creative universe is a solid enough foundation for a Jewish spiritual life.

At first, some elements of practice will feel clumsy because they call for skills, concepts, and tools that may be unfamiliar to you. Any initial awkwardness will diminish with practice as increasingly deeper aspects of the experience emerge. Because of the delicious and important sacred synergies that are possible, I encourage you to create a balanced menu of practices from each of the major dimensions of Judaism.

In this volume you will learn how to create meaningful, satisfying, stimulating Jewish experiences for yourself and those with whom you are connected that focus on the holy days and Shabbat. Subsequent volumes will empower you to travel equally deeply into the often hidden and strikingly profound meanings of, and methods for, confidently engaging yourself in G*d (shown in Hebrew in the center of the diagram on page xv); Prayer; Torah; Hebrew; Mitzvot, "sacred acts of consciousness"; Halahah, "ethics and norms"; Peoplehood; and Life-Cycle Events. It is my hope and intention that by the time you have finished you will have acquired a rich and well-rounded Jewish spiritual vocabulary.

Remember that this book is about reclaiming Judaism as a spiritual *practice*. You can taste each recipe, but it will take time for these practices to reach their full potential to change your life. If Judaism does truly have an effect that transcends belief, the benefits of these practices will gradually appear.

You might also want to visit the book's companion website, www.ReclaimingJudaism.org, where you will find additional practices and many more stories. There you can also listen to music; sample video clips; find others who might be teachers for you; and join affinity groups where you can talk about your Jewish experiences, innovations, and frustrations, and draw support to deepen your practice.

As your host rabbi, I'd like, before going any further, to offer a bit more in the way of introduction. I'm forty-eight as of this writing, the mother of two wonderful teenage sons, partner to my beloved second husband, Barry, stepmother to his three fascinating children, and Gramma Gohdie to their four children. My parents grew up Orthodox, we attended a Conservative synagogue, I became Orthodox in college, had a Reform boyfriend for many years, fell in love with Reconstructionism, went through a divorce, and, finding a need for spirituality in my life, was fortunate to discover the phenomenon known as Jewish renewal. Today I direct P'nai Yachadut, a research and training program that goes by the slogan "Meaning for Living through a Jewish Lens," and I write much of its website at www.ReclaimingJudaism.org. Through this aegis I travel internationally to mainstream communities and organizations to teach the reclaiming of Judaism. I also lead workshops at cutting-edge retreat centers like Esalen in Big Sur, California; Rancho La Puerta in Tecate, Mexico; and at the Jewish spiritual retreat center Elat Chayyim near Woodstock, New York.

As a rabbi I served almost ten years at Temple Beth El of Hammonton, New Jersey, and then for seven years as a dean of the transdenominational seminary The Academy for Jewish Religion. Before becoming a rabbi, I did research in biofeedback at the University of Pennsylvania, served as executive director of a Jewish

Federation, and invented, produced, and co-hosted the now popular public health television concept called *Health Watch*.

Probably best described as postdenominational, or "reconformadox," I am a graduate of the Reconstructionist Rabbinical College and have the privilege of the private *smi̱hah*, or ordination, of Rabbi Zalman Schachter-Shalomi, principal founder of Jewish renewal. I also hold a doctorate from New York Theological Seminary. My thesis was titled "Reframing Bar/Bat Mitzvah as a Rite of Spiritual Initiation"; an expanded version of that work is published in book form as *How to Make Your Own Bar/Bat Mitzvah*. In addition, I earned a master's degree in social work at Yeshiva University, a master's in Hebrew letters from the Reconstructionist Rabbinical College, and a bachelor's from the University of Pennsylvania. My teachers are capital and lowercase orthodox, conservative, reform, reconstructionist, renewal, agnostic, and atheist; scientists and mystics, as well as clergy and seekers of all faiths.

I am indebted to my teachers for their generosity and rigor. Most of us find ourselves united in our commitment to redeeming religion as a valuable part of the human experience. We all seem to have been created to help people discover the benefits of spirituality, and we all seem drawn to the task of taking religion to a new level. With profound respect for our inheritances, we are also innovators, working to make it possible to practice positive spirituality and create healthy religion that supports sane and safe civilization in a context of respectful pluralism. Since I am a Jew and a rabbi, the model offered here is Judaism, a Judaism that is designed to be inclusive, egalitarian, nonhierarchical, nontriumphalist, proactive for peace and justice, joyful, and healing.

Welcome to Reb Goldie's spiritual adventurers' club! You are now a member of the research and development team of the Jewish future. How you live what you taste, how you enhance it, advance it, and share it, will pour into the river that carries your light into the soul stream of Jewish history.

Go for it!

P.S. Please take note of three formatting decisions:

- I have chosen to represent the word *God* as G*d. This is to preserve the Jewish practice of approaching the Mysterious Evolving in which we are embedded with an attitude of humility, respect, and awe.
- Hebrew, Aramaic, and Yiddish have many words and word-roots in common. They also share letters that sound like you are clearing your throat, or trying to pronounce "khhh." Because the sound is often represented by the letter combination *ch*, many who rely on transliterations tend to sound out these words as if the *ch* were pronounced like the *ch* in the word *Chinese*, a sound that is not present in any of these three languages. Accordingly, this guttural *khhh* sound will be symbolized by an underlined letter <u>h</u> throughout this work.
- All translations are deliberately nonsystematic. They are phonetic, based on the way a term sounds to me and the way I believe it will be easiest for someone unaccustomed to Hebrew to sound it out during study, ritual, or prayer.

PART ONE

Reclaiming Holy Days

A blind man sits down next to a person having lunch on a park bench. The crunching sound is substantial and the blind man asks, "What is it that you are snacking on?" The woman having her lunch responds, "Oh, I'm so sorry. Please, let me give you some." She passes a sheet of matzah to the blind man. After many long moments of waiting to hear satisfied crunching, she breaks the silence and asks, "Is there a problem with it?" The blind man exclaims, "You must be kidding! Who wrote this nonsense?"

Perhaps your experience of the Jewish holidays is like that piece of matzah, cluttered with numerous traditions whose meaning is either elusive or seems too simplistic, something to do "for the children." Maybe you, too, have a relative who sits down, picks up the Haggadah, the guide for Passover seder rituals, grimaces, and declares: "Let's get this over with. We were enslaved, we escaped, we survived, we arrived, now let's eat." I, too, once felt like this, because I was wounded Jewishly from the boredom of experiences like rote reading out loud from a Maxwell House Haggadah.

In these pages you will learn how to infuse spiritual vitality into the Jewish holidays for yourself, your family, and your community. This goal requires the restoration of an essential ingredient that is found in the skills and concepts of applied spirituality. Passover, for example, is filled with birthing metaphors; the Hebrew word for Egypt, *Mitzrayim*, is based on its root, *maytzar*, which means "birth canal," "strait," or "narrow place." In your life, have you ever found yourself in a narrow place of oppression, dearly needing inspiration, longing to make a break for freedom? Was there also a "pharaoh consciousness" within you that prevented you from experiencing rebirth? Or perhaps someone else was playing the hardened pharaoh, making it impossible for you to continue to tolerate your work or living conditions? And if you did conquer your fear of change and plunge into the sea, did you emerge on the far shore a tender newborn, unclear about how to live in these new circumstances, wandering in the wilderness, discovering the importance of building a support system? Did you find yourself learning to live differently so that your hoped-for life in the promised land of your dreams might be realized?

Hidden in every Jewish holiday are nutrients and methods of preparation designed to help you delight in the gift of life by bringing you to ever-higher states of consciousness, joy, meaning, and intimacy. If, like me, you are part of the generation that was taught to rush through the rituals by rote, you may have been pushed along too fast to read the road signs of profound possibility that are posted on the Jewish holiday superhighway.

Holidays are composed of sequenced spiritual practices that, when taken seriously, will thicken with meaning and memories as you mature. Dressing in costume for Purim, for example, might at first seem like a way to engage the interest of children. But it can also serve as a jumping-off point for discussing what you might hope to do if placed in the position of Queen Esther, who had to choose whether to attempt to save the lives of her people by risking her own.

Just as a runner must stretch and strengthen his muscles before setting out, there are important practices to help you prepare practically, emotionally, intellectually, and spiritually for each Jewish holiday. I hope you taste them as well, because they will vastly deepen your ability to experience the full richness of the holidays.

The Passover Kiddush prayer includes the verse: *Z'man heyruteynu mikra kodesh*, "Times we are free holiness happens." The Jewish holidays are full of ways to help you to slow down and savor the meaning of life. Each holiday is rich in culture and character with its own unique symbols, setting, musical themes, prayers, rituals, stories, and foods. These themes and practices are intended to evoke discussion about the great questions of life both around your table and in your congregation so that all those present can learn from the past and, in turn, mentor one another.

THE FLOW OF SACRED TIME

The Jewish holidays are complementary and synergistic, so that each enriches the meaning of the next:

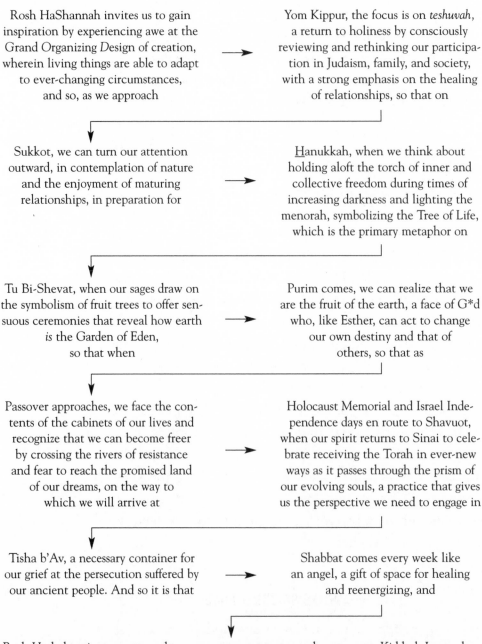

Rosh HaShannah invites us to gain inspiration by experiencing awe at the Grand Organizing Design of creation, wherein living things are able to adapt to ever-changing circumstances, and so, as we approach

Yom Kippur, the focus is on *teshuvah*, a return to holiness by consciously reviewing and rethinking our participation in Judaism, family, and society, with a strong emphasis on the healing of relationships, so that on

Sukkot, we can turn our attention outward, in contemplation of nature and the enjoyment of maturing relationships, in preparation for

Hanukkah, when we think about holding aloft the torch of inner and collective freedom during times of increasing darkness and lighting the menorah, symbolizing the Tree of Life, which is the primary metaphor on

Tu Bi-Shevat, when our sages draw on the symbolism of fruit trees to offer sensuous ceremonies that reveal how earth *is* the Garden of Eden, so that when

Purim comes, we can realize that we are the fruit of the earth, a face of G*d who, like Esther, can act to change our own destiny and that of others, so that as

Passover approaches, we face the contents of the cabinets of our lives and recognize that we can become freer by crossing the rivers of resistance and fear to reach the promised land of our dreams, on the way to which we will arrive at

Holocaust Memorial and Israel Independence days en route to Shavuot, when our spirit returns to Sinai to celebrate receiving the Torah in ever-new ways as it passes through the prism of our evolving souls, a practice that gives us the perspective we need to engage in

Tisha b'Av, a necessary container for our grief at the persecution suffered by our ancient people. And so it is that

Shabbat comes every week like an angel, a gift of space for healing and reenergizing, and

Rosh Hodesh arrives every month, a new moon ceremony, and so to comes Kiddush Levanah, a full moon ceremony, reminding us to gather together and remember that the cycles of nature are as important as our linear vision that people and civilizations will change for the better. The last month of the Jewish year, Elul, is filled with practices for engaging in a self-compassionate life review in preparation for the High Holy Days. And so the cycle of Jewish life begins anew.

Think of how the headlights of cars streaming along a dark highway become a loop of continuous light. The Jewish holidays are designed to help you sense the light of transformation traveling through your soul stream, cleansing it and adding vital nutrients. These sacred days can help you enjoy the safest and most expanded life possible, while also planting the seeds of even greater possibilities to be harvested by generations to come. Seen through the lens of ever-changing times, the value of the holy days endures, speaking ever-new volumes.

What is it like to really live in the cycle
of the Jewish Holy Days?
When Pesa<u>h</u>, Sukkot, or Shabbat come toward you,
are you aware of an anticipatory spiritual gusto?
How can the Jewish holy days
sweeten and deepen your journey?

MEMORIES IN EVERY MOUTHFUL

Just for the pleasure of it, open your mouth and taste the memory of noodle kugel, apple cake, gefilte fish. Inhale the aroma of *tzimmis*. Slip your choice of a dense or fluffy piece of matzah ball onto a spoon along with some golden chicken broth and bring it to your lips. Maybe your memories are more Sephardi, and you are recalling a chicken tagine or curry with apricots and almonds, some rosewater and candied citron.

The <u>h</u>allah is so golden, and this one has raisins and poppy seeds on top. You eat it with a bit of sweet butter. Not to mention the thought of crispy latkes with hot applesauce, and oh, oh, ohhh, are you thinking *cholent* and horseradish right now, or maybe it's matzah *brei*? And yes, with cinnamon, oh, cinnamon, and, well, if you insist, by all means pour a cup of sweet kosher blessing wine; it does seem to be in order.

Religious symbols are intentional spiritual catalysts. When considering holidays, the symbolic effect of food is very important. Jewish values, experience, and culture are at their most accessible through the metaphors embedded in taste, texture, and color. When the Passover ritual calls for eating *maror*, bitter horseradish, from the seder plate, we remember the bitterness in our lives; in the long, challenging life of the Jewish people; and in the lives of others on the planet. When ḥallah, apples, and honey are brought out to signify the turning over of the Jewish calendar year, and wishes for a sweet new year are called out, what memories do these foods conjure up for you?

When you are away from home,
or living in a new place,
or dining at someone else's table,
as you inhale the scent of holiday food,
are there memories in each spoonful?
Food and memory are a spiritual team.

Humans learn in a variety of ways, so the holidays are filled with pleasurable, multisensory ways of shaping sacred time and promoting the conscious evolution of humanity. Thus the Jewish holidays contain recipes for far more than food. Many of the holiday spiritual practices are designed to help lower the speed bumps in life—bumps constructed of the particular aspects of your character and relationships that trip you up year after year. Judaism has total faith in the human capacity to change for the better.

Can you imagine your life story expanding as your life experience, knowledge, and wisdom expand, so that, in the end, your life spiral, like that of the galaxies, blends into the flow of All Being? This metaphor is reflected in the Jewish holy day bread, hallah, which is braided for Shabbat and changes shape for the festivals and High Holy Days, when it becomes a spiral.

Have quantum leaps of personal and communal transformation not always been your Jewish holiday experience? Understood. I have shared your frustration. It is time to recover some of the inheritance you were meant to receive. In the following pages we will unwind many of the powerful holy day metaphors and symbols in order to grasp the underlying meaning of these spiritual practices and become better able to savor their benefits.

Jewish holy days have little in common
with going to the mall,
watching the stock market fluctuate,
betting on a ball game,
working overtime at the office,
or doing homework after school.
They are about a (w)holy other way of using time.

The nutrients you can bring
to your soul stream through
Jewish holiday preparation and celebration
act like tiny spiritual time capsules that continue
to improve the week ("weak") days of your life.

Through these practices, you will mature and stretch yourself over the years, refining your ability to access the many delicious flavors of your humanity.

RECIPE # 1
Seder *Yehi Ratzon*—A Sephardi Blessing Feast

Symbolic foods and their blessings richly inform the Sephardi Rosh HaShannah dinner tradition. Sephardi Jews offer blessings while holding up a plate with the foods listed below as a dinner table ritual. Some prefer individual plates for each of the following:

- Date
- Pomegranate
- Pumpkin
- Leek
- Beet root
- Fish (a whole fish or a fish head)
- Apples
- Honey

It is also customary to serve dishes made of these foods as part of the festival meal. Each item is blessed in the order given below, and after the blessing, all respond *ameyn* and eat a bit of the item. *Ameyn* can been seen as an acronym for *El* (G*d), *meleh* (King, or Governing Principle of the universe), *neh-eh-mahn* (faithful). Feel free to invite improvisation on the blessings from those present.

FOR THE DATE: May this sweet date bring a year of sweetness, happiness, blessing, and peace for all beings.

POMEGRANATE: In the year to come, may we be able to manifest good deeds, just as this pomegranate is filled with seeds symbolizing the 613 mitzvot in the Torah.

SLICED APPLES DRENCHED IN HONEY: Grant us a crisp new year of sweet, sweet life! As the prophet Nehemiah said: "Go eat rich dishes and drink sweet drinks, and send portions to those who have nothing ready, for today is holy to our G*d. Do not mourn, for your strength is in being joyful to the Lord."

PUMPKIN, OR SQUASH: May the coming year grow as full with blessing as a gourd grows full with seed. As a gourd grows firm with time, so may we be protected on our journey through life in this New Year.

LEEKS: May good luck be ours in the year to come!

BEET ROOT: Those who would do us evil, may they be defeated and repent their ways.

FISH: May our journey be toward You and Your ways of peace. May we be blessed with forward thinking and a life filled with health and happiness.

Let us all say: *Ameyn!*

Understanding the High Holy Day Season

Personal awareness and the refinement of your self as a conscious agent in life are the primary themes of the High Holy Day season. Life has chosen you, it flows through you, and the self that you cultivate will shape that life. The power of the Jewish belief in every person's ability to attain desired change is so great that Rabbi Adin Steinsaltz has described it as the ability to "overleap" your past.

The High Holy Days involve a sequence of practices of life review that allow for an annual experience of spiritual rebirth. These include:

- Pausing to listen to your wake-up calls by blowing the shofar, a ram's horn, during Elul, the lunar month that precedes the High Holy Days.
- Active interpersonal efforts to initiate healing in relationships. This process is called *teshuvah*.
- A routine of empathic introspection termed *heshbon hanefesh*.

- *Viduii*, an admission of individual and collective responsibility for the consequences of our acts through a sequence of awareness-raising prayers and a late-night service known as *seli̱hot*.
- A ritual to help release obstacles to desired change, *tashli̱h*.
- Encounters with specific Torah portions that raise vital relationship issues.
- And, upon reaching Yom Kippur, *tzom*, "fasting," as a way to support your total focus on the spiritual rather than the physical.
- Breaking the fast, a meal of revival, celebrating your entry into a renewed life.

SHOFAR YOURSELF

Do your wake-up calls happen in difficult ways? A spouse leaves—that is often termed a wake-up call. A teenager is arrested for drug possession. Someone ignoring the heavy stresses that require attention in life is involved in a car accident. Wake-up calls all. Judaism offers the equivalent of a spiritual alarm clock, wake-up calls embedded in spiritual time so you won't have to be hit over the head so often by your life.

The High Holy Days are the apex of passion in Jewish spiritual time. As loudly as they can possibly speak to you through the medium of religious traditions, your ancestors are trying to draw your attention to crucial, yet not necessarily visible, issues in your life. On Rosh HaShannah and at the conclusion of Yom Kippur, the shofar, a ram's horn, is blown. It is also traditional to begin to prepare yourself for the High

Holy Days by blowing a daily blast on the shofar at home and at services for the entire month prior to Rosh HaShannah except on the Sabbath.

The sound of the shofar is spiritually riveting. It symbolizes the wake-up call from "an angel" that Abraham received. Believing that it was the will of G*d, Abraham had already set his son Isaac on an altar for sacrifice when he heard a voice telling him not to hurt the child. Looking up, he noticed a ram caught in a thicket nearby, which he substituted for the boy.

That ram's horn has traveled symbolically through time
as the shofar,
coming to symbolize a spiritual wake-up call:
"Where are you? Wake up! What are you doing?
Look at what *you* are about to sacrifice."

T'kee-ah! Sh'vareem! T'ru-ah!
Around the planet service leaders chant
these onomatopoeic Hebrew musical commands
to call forth one hundred blasts
of the shofar on Rosh HaShannah.
One hundred chances for you to really listen for
the messages that are trying to reach you.

Let the sound pierce through you.
It comes across thousands of years to your ears,
from the time when the first breath of
life awoke the first human form.
From when it became clear that even Abraham
had to learn to listen.

From the flood, in the wake of which even
G*d decided to repent,
realizing that design flaws in humans were no
defense for our slaughter.

With each blast, you might ask yourself:
"Is there more to listen for in my life?

"Are my actions/decisions/thoughts off base?
What do I really know?
What do I feel?
What might I do differently this time?"

RECIPE # 2
Setting the
Alarm for
Your Wake-
Up Call

For personal contemplation or discussion with a best friend:

- Have you had a wake-up call this year? in life?
- Is there someone in your life who needs a wake-up call?
- Abraham is alerted to his horrific folly by an "angel," a *mahlah*. Are you meant to be a *mahlah* for someone in your life? How will you sound the necessary wake-up call? Who has been a *mahlah* for you?
- In the long run, did a painful call ever awaken you to a whole new life?
- If, at home, you were to introduce *daily* shofar-blowing during the month prior to the High Holy Days, could you imagine the looks on the faces of those around you?

• What explanation would you give that might help someone else listen to the shofar and derive meaning from the moment?

If you forget to blow the shofar during one of the days of Elul, don't berate yourself. Notice what it felt like to miss that day, recommit to your intentions, and continue the practice. Imagine a month of listening for wake-up calls, so that you can act on them before they act on you.

FORGIVENESS PRACTICE

Too often people face
the ark,
the leader,
the teacher,
the television,
the monitor,
the game.
Too little do we
face each other.
Or even know how.

Developing sustainable, meaningful intimacy
is one important theme of the Jewish Holy Days.

Intimacy with all people,
the Jewish people,
nature,
the planet,
and the Source of Life.

Judaism does not offer a doctrine of unconditional forgiveness from G*d. Any hurt you have dealt another human being can be forgiven only by working it through with that person. One of the most powerful of Jewish spiritual practices is called *teshuvah,* which comes from the root word *shuv,* "turn." The goal of *teshuvah* practice is to create a healthy shift in the negative energy flowing between you and an experience, a person, or the Source of Life. That is our route to transformation.

You may have made mistakes at one time or another that now evoke feelings of great dismay and shame. You may also have borne the brunt of unforgivable acts committed by others. There are, indeed, people in whose presence it may be utterly unsafe to place yourself. Even so, it is still possible to begin a process of changing the way you regard those people and what they did that will reduce the power of what happened to hold sway over you. Sometimes you will create this *teshuvah* process directly with another person; at other times, because he is deceased or dangerous to you, it must be done in his absence.

To become adept at *teshuvah* is to attain one of the greatest of the Jewish life skills. You will be able to walk across a room and avoid fewer people; you'll be able to serve on committees, or attend parties and family gatherings without the stress that comes from knowing you have unfinished business with someone who might be present. *Teshuvah* is a process for turning a new face toward a situation and engaging in a process of gradual healing. Let's begin with the case of someone you can, at least in theory, approach. Before you initiate this practice, it helps to have a formula in place that is comfortable on your lips:

Sandra? This is Reb Goldie. I feel there is some negative energy between us. I'd love to listen to your point of view about what has happened. I promise not to respond defensively, to really just listen and learn. If you would be open to it, I'd like us to start a process that might lead to a better relationship between us. This is too important to get into on the telephone; would you be open to setting a date for a meeting?

Rather than triggering fears of abandonment, asking for a *teshuvah* session shows that you want to repair, not destroy the relationship. It is an indication of commitment. However, do not assume when asking someone to engage in this practice that she will agree to it or be emotionally available to do so. Do understand that simply asking the question begins the process, because even if no face-to-face meeting takes place, the seed of possibility has been planted. You have engaged in a sacred first step and done your best.

Try not to leap from engaging in an important or stressful activity directly into a *teshuvah* session. It is important to arrive centered, grounded, slowed down, and available to listen. Engaging in a meditation walk en route to a *teshuvah* session can be an excellent form of preparation. This practice is intended to help release your thoughts, expectations, and anxieties about the upcoming *teshuvah* session.

    A meditation walk is done slowly enough that you become conscious of each part of every footstep. Let time slow down, the present become everything, the step gone by not as

RECIPE # 3
Teshuvah:
Forgiveness
Walks

important as the one in which you are engaged. As thoughts intrude, and they will, notice them with an internal "Ah yes, of course, someone in my position would be feeling that way," and release them gently, returning to your foot-centered consciousness. It is helpful to repeat a sacred phrase during such walks. I recommend a verse from Torah: *L'hith̲ale̲h lifnei Elohim*, which means to "Walk yourself before G*d."

RECIPE # 3
A *Teshuvah* Rehearsal

Is there someone with whom you desire to do *teshuvah*?

- Imagine that you are heading to the front door of the person with whom you wish to do *teshuvah*.
- Prepare yourself to issue the *teshuvah* invitation.
- Imagine the door opening, the person standing there.
- How are you received? Place what you learn from this rehearsal into your spiritual treasure chest of awareness.
- Begin walking again. Arrive at this person's door in your imagination yet a second time. Notice all the images your mind projects about how the person might act, and continue rehearsing until you are simply curious about how he will react. You won't know until you try.

A GRADUAL MATTER

The first *teshuvah* session rarely completes the healing, but it *is* a new beginning, a rebirth of potential for movement within the relationship. You may have experienced what I call "cheap *teshuvah*," done in a hollow, formulaic phone call. *Real teshuvah* takes time. My husband, Barry, taught me early on to "give the rough places we are working on together time to evolve. Let's engage in this for a while, then back off to allow deepening and healing, and reengage another day to reach the next level." Not quick, not cheap, but deep.

Rebuilding trust is a very long process. By listening without judgment, you will discover many facts about the situation that were previously unknown to you; inaccurate assumptions made on both your parts will often be revealed. This is not about right or wrong; it is about reaching a new level of understanding. Doing *teshuvah* with someone is one way to experience pure holiness. With practice it becomes much easier.

Rabbi Shlomo Carlbach taught that *teshuvah* can be so all-encompassing that the original error will seem to be erased from history. Would that all of us could wake up soon enough, be strong enough, and live long enough to erase such wrinkles in the fabric of time!

WHAT ABOUT THE UNFORGIVABLE?

When I teach *teshuvah* workshops, an important question that inevitably gets raised is this: "Do I have to forgive? What about in cases of abuse?" The answer may surprise you. There are clear criteria about what constitutes genuine *teshuvah*:

- Admission of a reprehensible act without rationalizations or excuses.
- Remorse, being truly sorry and regretful.
- Genuine commitment to not repeating the act.

- Getting the help required for constructive personal change.

There is something very positive you can do for someone who has been unable to change or repent or for someone who has died before she was able to do so. The Talmud cites a teaching about Rabbi Meir, who had prayed for highway robbers in the neighborhood to be struck down. His wife, Beruria, corrected him, saying, "Rather, pray for them to repent" (Berahot 10a). So, too, we can pray for those who have hurt us to lose that compulsion in this life, or, if they have died, on the next plane of being. If their souls do return to life on this planet, we can pray for them to be free of such terrible compulsions, that they might have a new experience of life and that no more people might be hurt by them. This is a new kind of *teshuvah* for many of us. To turn anger, once we've had sufficient time to vent and process it over the years, into prayer. This is a way not to forgive but rather to turn a new face to an old wound so that the scar can be resurfaced and healing can tentatively begin.

And what if you have wronged someone who will not accept your *teshuvah?* Maimonides suggests bringing three character witnesses with you to entreat forgiveness, and to do this up to three times. If after that the person you have wronged still does not accept your *teshuvah*, the burden of guilt transfers to the one who will not forgive. And what if the person wronged dies before you are able to confess your culpability? Again Maimonides has the answer. At the grave of the person you have wronged, assemble ten people who recognize the depth of your *teshuvah* and express it out loud as if the deceased could hear. If the situation also involves money you owe the deceased, give it to the heirs, and if there are no heirs, to a bona fide charity.

The Jewish New Year is not approached with resolutions.
It is the spirit of our practice
to initiate real change immediately,
to begin the dynamics of transformation long before
the closing gates of Yom Kippur,
when you will seal a season of your life filled with
the intended and unintended consequences of
words, choices, and decisions gone by.

ARE ALL RESPONSIBLE?

Jews take collective responsibility for the moral targets that get missed in life. At least ten days before Rosh HaShannah, we add a prayer practice called *seli̱hot*, in which, having empathy for ourselves as being only human, we admit personal and collective ownership of the full range of problematic human behaviors. Let's look at a few verses from one of the *Seli̱hot* prayers, the *Ashamnu:*

Ashamnu	*We are guilty* (spiritually desolate and distant from our higher selves)
Bagadnu	*We have betrayed* (our loved ones, the community, the planet)
Gazalnu	*We have stolen* (eaten without giving thanks; removed the rights, privacy and dignity of others)
Dibarnu dofi	*We have spoken slander* (spoken behind others' backs, discrediting them)

A congregant of mine once protested, asking why, since he lived such a careful life, he should recite lines of wrongdoings that did not apply to him? The answer, in the words of Rabbi

Abraham Joshua Heschel, is that "In a democratic society, not all are guilty, but indeed all are responsible."

Think, for example, about environmentalism. There is a synergy between the one paper cup of yours that you throw into the trash container and all the cups tossed to the ground by those who came before you. When awareness of the impact of environmentally irresponsible practices knocks on a single heart, it often awakens the desire for collective responsibility. Judaism looks upon the planet much like a glorious national park that should be thoroughly enjoyed while also being treated with great respect and appreciation.

As the High Holy Days approach, the passion for knowing yourself and acknowledging missteps intensifies. While people tend to think of *viduii*, "confession," as a Christian practice, it has long been a part of Judaism as well, although the precise nature of our confession is different. Our confessional prayers do not specify each error as an *aveyrah*, "sin," but rather as a *heyt*, an archery term meaning "a missed mark." Judaism understands you to be constantly developing and capable of changing your trajectory. Jewish spiritual practices encourage you to take moral targets seriously and to work to improve your aim, because the consequences of your intentions, words, works, and actions are like the proverbial pebble yielding endless ripples in the life of your communities of influence.

Make a fist with one hand.
Use it to softly knock on the door to your heart
while reciting the moral targets you
and other humans likely missed this year.
"Al heyt shehatahnu l'fanehah,"
regarding the mark *we* have missed . . .

You are not alone in facing this hard part of being human.
Look around you in synagogue.
We are all culpable, interdependent, struggling.

We all can evolve; we all can change. One central metaphor of the High Holy Day season is to reflect and pray as if these were the last days of your life. For some, this creates a sense of urgency for understanding and change, and they will penitentially thump themselves over the heart with a closed fist. The Kotsker Rebbe, a nineteenth-century Ḥasidic master, suggested a gentle massage over the heart area during the powerful confessional litanies. For a new year to be even more full of life than the previous one, there is much understanding to be gained from the days you have already lived.

Everywhere a Jew is praying, we are re-remembering together the human obligation to be custodians of the earth, of ethics, and of peace. Yes, we are culpable if we stand by idly and don't intervene when we see someone fall short of his mark. And, *you* don't have to do it all on your own; we all are teammates. Judaism views all humans as team members in the great research and development project known as creation. This project began long before you emerged and hopefully will continue long after you depart. In *Pirkei Avot*, "Ethics of the Fathers," our sages put it this way: "It is not incumbent upon you to complete the task; nor are you free to desist from it."

In every generation, the prayers and practices of Judaism are updated to reflect the times in which our lives are embedded. Here is a current example. Each line was written by a different

RECIPE # 4
Missing the
Mark

member of Temple Beth El of Hammonton, New Jersey, during a workshop we did together titled "Immersing Ourselves in the Emotions of the High Holidays."

> *Al heyt shehatahnu l'fanehah* For the mark we have missed
>   before You:
> By neglecting the trees,
> By coming home too late from work each day,
> By keeping silent in the face of evil,
> By spending more on excess possessions than on helping others,
> By not listening to our children,
> By working on Shabbat instead of resting with family,
> By not sufficiently visiting or calling our parents.
> *V'al kulam, Elohai selihot, slah lah-nu, m'hal lah-nu, kah-pehr
>   lah-nu.*

For all of these, G*d of forgiveness, excuse us, pardon us, atone [with] us.

(Note that the word *atone* = *at one*; be at one with us.)

- During Elul, sit down with your congregation, study group, or family. Provide copies of the *Al Heyt* litany from a traditional *mahzor*, "High Holy Day prayer book," as a model for study.
- Ask those present to compose a personal list of the missed marks about which they feel most keenly this year. Then go around the room asking each person to share one of her own.
- Keep a master list on a big board or sheet in front of the group. Continue going around until the group feels satisfied that it has compiled a complete list for this moment in time.

- Recite the list together while tapping on the door
  to your hearts. Take note of the traditional refrain
  above and perhaps chant it between couplets of the
  Al <u>H</u>eyt you wrote together.

You might save this community Al <u>H</u>eyt to recite again at Yom Kippur services in addition to the traditional Al <u>H</u>eyt. Then, each year, your community can regather during Elul to fine-tune the awareness of what is knocking on your collective hearts. Think about how you personally, as well as through communal social action committees, might follow up with programs to address these newly emerging issues.

PREPARING THE SURFACE OF YOUR LIFE

In the Torah, Rosh HaShannah is called Yom HaZikaron, "a Day for Remembering" the miracle of creation. It is considered to be the birthday of the world, the beginning of calendar time, the ultimate New Year. But Rosh HaShannah also has another name, Yom HaDin, the "Day of Judgment," which reflects another aspect of its character.

"A Day of Judgment!
What kind of New Year is that?"
you might well exclaim.

Din is the ability to really look at yourself
and compassionately begin to realign your soul.
Craving a smoother journey? With maturity,
you may begin to desire din, to learn from it
in order to be a healthier participant in life.

The ten days from Rosh HaShannah through Yom Kippur are termed the *Yamim No'rah'im,* "Days of Awe," during which it is a practice to feel that you are participating in a divine review of your ethical actions. Being only human, you will have errors on your record, and so it helps to have a sense that you will earn "extra credit" on your examination by having made a sincere effort at introspection and personal change during the year that has passed. Many people think of Yom Kippur, the "Day of Atonement," as the annual focus of repentance practice. In reality, however, it is the culmination of an entire year's cycle of serious self-reflection.

The process of determining with whom you hope to engage in *teshuvah* is but one aspect of the practice known as *heshbon hanefesh,* doing "an accounting of the soul." There are many days in the calendar—such as Thursday evenings, as part of lifting "soul *shmutz*" in preparation for Shabbat, and the day before each new moon, which is known as Yom Kippur Katan, "Little Yom Kippur"—when incremental *heshbon hanefesh* work is traditionally practiced. It is, however, most effective when engaged in nightly. Instead of extricating yourself from daily life and plunging directly into the High Holy Days, a regular *heshbon hanefesh* practice will help you to arrive prepared.

In 1812 Rabbi Mendel of Satanov published a new approach to *heshbon hanefesh,* an eighteen-step program comprising journaling, self-reflection, and planned personal change based on specific characteristics, such as decisiveness, economic stability, and silence. This process is described beautifully by Alan Morinis in his book, *Climbing Jacob's Ladder.* In the next recipe, however, I am going to use Reb Mendel's categories to introduce a different approach, one based on my own studies with Dr. Gene Gendlin, the author of *Focusing*.

In order to be truly free, we need to look honestly and compassionately into sensitive areas of the self. It is important to bring something comforting with you as you enter this process. I sometimes hold onto the memory of my mentor Louise P. Vanett, whose advice was so full of love and respect that I could trust and absorb her guidance with little resistance. Having our cat on my lap is quite comforting during such a practice as well.

RECIPE # 5
An Accounting of the Soul via the Body

- Take any one of the qualities listed below and engage in an initial reflection on its degree of presence and activity in your life.
- Next, you might sit with a friend, a partner, a class, or a child and discuss the quality. Give examples of how it is manifested. Flesh out its meaning for yourself; find as many nuances as you can.

These are the qualities Reb Mendel identified, paired with my interpretation of one of their possible meanings:

Equanimity	The ability to live in balance
Tolerance	Accepting challenges with respect and curiosity
Orderliness	Allocating time for living life fully with integrity

Decisiveness	Acting promptly when your reasoning is sure
Cleanliness	Modeling dignity in your ways and space
Humility	Knowing you will always have much to learn and more opinions than answers
Righteousness	Conducting your life in such a way that you will be trusted and respected
Economic Stability	Safeguarding enough resources for yourself to live without debt
Zeal	Living with gusto focused on purpose and care
Silence	Listening and reflecting before speaking
Calmness	Describing your needs and thoughts gently while being respectful and clear
Truth	Speaking only what is fully confirmed as fact
Separation	Focusing on each aspect of your daily life in its own time, rather than multitasking
Temperance	Eating and drinking for good health, not dangerous excess
Deliberation	Pausing before acting, considering consequences, integrating heart and mind wisely
Modest Ways	Eschewing crude, lewd, and boastful mannerisms and practices
Trust	Living in the spirit of knowing there is abundance in the universe and you are in the flow
Generosity	Finding satisfaction in making much possible for others

- Now, turn your focus inward and notice whether in your body a memory from the story of your life is resonating with the quality you have chosen. The mind/body connection creates a shortcut to knowing. Is a message from deep in your memory lodged somewhere? Perhaps a twinge in the back, tension in your neck, the dawning of a huge smile of pleasure, or a relaxing of your shoulders. Rather than thinking about the quality, listen to the memory; discover what your body knows about it. Then, take the information, gently set it before you, and return to see if there is more, something new you can learn inside yourself.

An example that comes up for me concerns the quality of deliberation. One day I hurt my sister's feelings deeply by describing a best friend as being like a sister to me. While I didn't intend to hurt, her misunderstanding was something I might have anticipated, had I spoken with greater deliberation. This memory emerged when I read the phrase above about deliberation and then noticed a sinking feeling in my stomach. While visiting this feeling in my body, the memory arose full-blown, as if it had happened only yesterday.

- What is your desire with regard to the memory that surfaced in relation to the quality you are contemplating? Sit quietly with this question until a variety of possibilities arise. Your first thought may feel very strong and true; look under it for softer voices. A greater truth usually lies beneath the loudest voices we hear inside. Invite strength and support for your intention from the great dynamic flow of all possibilities in creation.

To continue with the example above, while my first thought was to try yet one more new way to get my sister to understand, underneath that thought was the knowledge that only she could elect to transform her own feelings. Instead, this memory strengthened my resolve to pause and think before speaking, to practice what I preach, so that the consequences of lacking deliberation will be lessened in my life.

FREEING BLOCKAGES

Practices like *heshbon hanefesh*, shofar blowing, reciting lists of marks you've missed, and engaging in *teshuvah* are likely to bring into focus unresolved issues and obstacles to healing. Are you renewing hurts you might be ready to release? I once saw graffiti on a wall that said: "Resentments are like stray cats. If you keep feeding them they won't go away." On the second day of Rosh HaShannah one often finds individual Jews and entire communities heading down to oceans, lakes, and rivers to engage in *tashlih*, an ancient ritual of compressing what needs to be let go within crumbs of bread and then casting into the water the sticky points within memories, personae, and relationships that are getting in the way of creating a better new year.

Tashlih, meaning "You will cast away," is an experience whereby you symbolically enact what you hope to better understand or transform. Most sources date this ritual to the fourteenth century, although in the Bible, in the writings of the prophet Micah, one finds a possible earlier reference: "You forgive sins and overlook missteps . . . and You will cast into the depths of the sea all their errors." Good ritual facilitates desired change and provides one more way to empower yourself in the direction of your hopes.

The public nature of *tashlih* can have important, unanticipated effects. One year in Amsterdam, darkness was descending as we chanted Rabbi Shefa Gold's prayer for *tashlih*:

> Wash over me, carry my prayers to
> a G*d who hears.
> Wash over me, send me an answer
> to my tears.
> I cast out my worries, I cast out my fears.

Several hundred strong, we made our way to the canal. Holland is a difficult place to be Jewish, and as we lined the streets of the old ghetto with our gentle chanting, one congregant angrily asked how I could dare to take a group of Jews into the streets. "We don't do this. Since the war, no column of Jews has walked these streets. In columns, this was how we were taken to the camps." Beside her, a young man turned. "Momma, that is why this is the most beautiful day. Look, we are still here, still taking ourselves to the water to purify our intentions, to take seriously changing ourselves for the better. Look at the neighbors. Imagine if they would join us. They have much to purify in themselves. Better they see that we are still here, growing stronger every day, and that we still believe it is possible to change the world, starting with ourselves!"

RECIPE # 6
Growing Up
with Spiritual
Support:
Tashliḥ with
Children

The Locher family in Holland taught me a lovely method for doing *tashliḥ* that works well in the presence and with the participation of children.

- Near a body of water, distribute bits of bread.
- Ask each child to think of some quality in himself that he is working on.
- Invite her to call out that quality while throwing the bit of bread up into the air over the water.
- Everyone witnessing this act then calls out ways that quality might be transformed.

For example, if the young person calls out "lies," a transformation word or phrase might be "truth," or "asking for what you need," or "clear explanations." Or, if the young person calls out "temper tantrums," those who are gathered call out "telling your strong feelings" or other transformations full of wisdom. This can combine fun with teaching the desire for change in the presence of a supportive family and community.

THE TORAH OF RELATIONSHIPS

On Rosh HaShannah, the Jewish calendar changes in accordance with a date originally calibrated to coincide with what the ancients perceived to be the "birthday of the world." Rosh HaShannah is observed for two days because of the problems created by using the time of the new moon to establish precisely the turn of the year, and because once the date had been established, the news took time to communicate around the world. While precise dating no longer requires moon sightings, we continue the practice of observing Rosh HaShannah for two days because the spiritual nutrients conveyed on this holiday take time to digest. In addition to the *yirah*, "awe," engendered by contemplating the birthing of creation, the Torah readings for these two days offer a sobering study in the human uses of power.

Each Rosh HaShannah Torah reading
contains extreme stories of traumatic family incidents
that are depicted as sanctioned by G*d.
One is caused by Sarah, the other by Abraham.
Both affect the children, the parents, and future generations.
Why? How is this part of starting a new year?

In the Torah reading for the first day of Rosh HaShannah, Sarah has been unable to conceive, and, following regional custom, gives her handmaid Hagar to Abraham to bear him children. So Hagar gives birth to Abraham's firstborn son, Ishmael. Very late in life, Sarah does bear Abraham a son, Isaac. After Isaac's viability is ensured (marked by a weaning celebration), Sarah demands that Abraham expel his firstborn son, as well as the boy's mother (with whom Abraham has perhaps grown too close).

In the ensuing scene, Hagar has been cast into the desert. Her water sack is now empty, and she is sitting in a state of acute depression. She sets her son down in the shade, "a bow shot" away from her. She cannot even lift her head to realize that a well is within sight; she has lost everything. At a substantial distance, perhaps out of her son's hearing range, Hagar becomes able to "raise her voice" to G*d. It will then take what the Torah terms "an angel calling out from the heavens" to get her to look up, to help her find promise in her situation.

Hagar's ability to pray in extremis is found in the Torah reading for the first day of Rosh HaShannah. As Hagar begins to see a bigger, better picture for her future, and to feel connected to the flow of a greater destiny that dwarfs the immediate disaster, her eyes are opened to her place in the great unfolding story of time and creation. So, too, we are given the opportunity to lift our voices and connect with a new vision on Rosh HaShannah as well as on any day when we allow ourselves to pour out our hearts before G*d.

Hagar and her son are survivors. Even so, how long do they wander in an angry daze? What is the legacy of Hagar's trauma for future generations? Some Arab tribes believe that they are descendants of Ishmael; consider the implication of that belief for relationships between Arabs and Jews.

If you could rewrite the Torah, how would you have Sarah and Hagar behave toward one another? What would you want to say to Abraham about his role in the drama? How do we so easily lose sight of the well, of the abundance that fills creation? Who was the angel who helped Hagar to look up? Could it have been Sarah, who slipped out of her tent to repent, to bring her water, to ask her to return? Did they talk? Did Hagar elect not to return? Why?

Abraham's younger son, Isaac, may seem to have his future ensured once his mother clears out the competition. But now, in addition to the trauma of losing his older brother and Hagar's caring presence, Isaac, too, will be severely traumatized. It is in the reading for the second day of Rosh HaShannah, known as the *Akedah*, that Abraham believes G*d has instructed him to show his faith by sacrificing Isaac on a mountaintop.

Like Hagar, Abraham will also need to "hear" differently in order to envision a different outcome. Again it will take "an angel calling out from the heavens" to make him aware of an alternate reality. Only after Abraham has bound Isaac to the altar and raised the sacrificial knife will he notice the ram that has become snagged by its horns in the bushes and understand that there is a holy alternative to killing his son.

These are New Year texts because they express
the power to transform
that comes from connecting to the
Endless Flow of Possibility.
The experience can fill you,
as Hagar filled her flask and Abraham stilled his hand,
with the spiritual energy you need to live your life.

These Torah portions are also
intended to help you sift through your own life,
to put a stop to the possible traumas you, too,
might be handing down through the generations.

The shattering of relationships in these stories is profound. Isaac will not travel back down the mountain in the company of his father, and neither he nor his brother appears to be at the funeral of Sarah, or, it would seem, at Abraham's later remarriage to Keturah. You will never again find a discussion between this father and his sons in the Torah. After the *Akedah*, Abraham and Sarah reside in different cities, and there is no biblical evidence that they ever meet or speak again. Abraham will travel to gather Sarah's bones for burial. Ishmael and Isaac are next seen together when they meet at

Abraham's funeral, although the Torah does not tell us whether they spoke to one another. Even so, Isaac is never far from Abraham's thoughts. He will send his servant to subtly ensure that his son finds a proper wife and at the end of his life he will send both Ishmael and the children he bore with Keturah away with departure gifts and then leave "all that was his" to Isaac (Genesis 25:6).

The sages have written about what this story meant to them. Most were impressed by the strength of Abraham's faith. Israeli scholar Dr. Aviva Zornberg points out that in the classical midrash (rabbinic commentaries provided to fill gaps in the text) some describe the agonized sound of the shofar as expressing Sarah's incredulity and horror at what Abraham had attempted to do. Some say it killed Sarah to hear of her child's narrow escape from death and that the wail of the shofar brings to our ears her last cry of agony. The Torah, however, leaves Sarah voiceless on the matter. When in the end Isaac inherits all that was Abraham's, including the covenant, does Ishmael feel wounded by his father yet again? In his book *Jewish Renewal*, Rabbi Michael Lerner suggests a repetition compulsion at work here, a deeply destructive family pattern being revealed. We wonder: Can it be stopped? transformed? And then we realize that is up to us, the heirs, to create transformation.

In Judaism, even moments of colossal terror and injustice are included in a document that is considered holy. The same is true for your life. Every stitch of every moment is part of your holiness, depending on your perspective. The ancestors seem to have purposefully passed to you a scroll full of dysfunctional families acting out all over the place, so that you might discover new possibilities, as Abraham did, and so that you might learn from the mistakes of your ancestors and thus diminish your own inclination to misstep.

YIZKOR: THE SACRED ART OF REMEMBERING

Perhaps you had occasion to be at Yom Kippur services as a child. If so, you may remember a time when all the children were quietly ushered out of the room. *Yizkor* was about to start. The root of *Yizkor* is *zahor,* memory. This personal *Yizkor,* the deepest remembering of loved ones who have died, is offered during the major festivals: on the last day of Sukkot, the last day of Passover, and the second day of Shavuot.

On Yom Kippur, however, we also remember all the martyrs of the Jewish people. The prayer *Eleh Ez-k'rah* embodies a partial listing of the tragic, terrifying deaths of those whose crime was simply to be Jewish. The killers, those who tried to destroy the pathways to (w)holiness retained in the collective memory of the Jewish people, are not the focus; instead, the martyrs themselves are emphasized in the prayers. An awakening of intense magnitude is made possible during these recitations, because it becomes clear that

> Despite the Crusades, the Spanish Inquisition,
> the Chmielnicki massacres, pogroms, and the Holocaust,
> the Jewish people are one of the longest-existing
> civilizations on the planet.

> We are stem cells on behalf of Creation's efforts
> to build the future,
> trying to get past our own creatureliness
> to help holiness happen within humanity,

and always at risk from those who fear change,
who would inhibit the process.

We remember, we mourn,
and we derive strength from standing beside one another.
We're still here, being of service, as we are meant to be.

Yizkor moves from the collective to the individual. Around the room, eyes brim with tears as those who stood beside us, held us, hurt us, and led us are remembered. We feel very close to them at this time when awareness of our vulnerability, our missed marks, and our hopes for contributing better selves to the creation of a better world combine. They seem to be within hearing distance as the gates of time stand open on this day of profound introspection. We realize we are not alone in this life from which one cannot get out alive; all share the experience of loss. The minor key of the sacred music throbs like a voice, for most of us cannot speak as we honor the memory of those who have left this plane of being. Then, all softly say the Mourner's Kaddish and remember the holiness of a loving touch.

The instinct to shield children from death and sadness is understandable. Still, experts encourage us to teach them resilience by allowing our youth to learn how to mourn, to realize that life is a series of ups and downs.

RECIPE # 7
Remembering
Those You've
Loved and Lost   Select a group of photographs of those in your family and personal life who have passed on.

- Set up a tray of water (for safety) in which you will place a thick white *yahrzeit* (memorial) candle set in glass for each first-degree relative who has died during your lifetime (siblings, parents, aunts, uncles; some also include grandparents and dear friends). Candles that will burn for a full day are sold in Jewish specialty stores for this purpose.
- Set the photos out around the tray.
- The evening when Yom Kippur begins is known as *erev* Yom Kippur. (*Erev* means "evening," and Jewish days begin at sunset.) At this time, gather your family to light the *yahrzeit* candles.
- After candlelighting, give a photo to each of your children, or your nieces/nephews, or students, or someone you are mentoring. If you are able to, share a story about the life of that person at this time, something that really conveys why remembering this person means so much to you.
- If the children knew the person, they might have stories to share, too. Invite them to ask questions and share your feelings, and ask them to express theirs. Let them know it is a good thing to remember loved ones, and that sad feelings often exist alongside happy and difficult memories. Let them know that to honor and remember a soul in this way is a precious part of being Jewish.
- Ask the children and young people to join you in honoring the memory of the person whose photo they are holding by attending the *Yizkor* service on Yom Kippur day. You might also choose to include historical figures such as Hannah Senesh,

Anne Frank, and Yitzhak Rabin. When it is the children's turn to experience a palpable, personal loss, you will have taught them how to begin to derive support from these deep traditions.

- Remember to write names and dates on all those family photographs. Identify yourself as well. Someday someone may be remembering you.

DISTINCTIONS

In your mind, are there clear differences between Rosh HaShannah and Yom Kippur? Many people recall them as quite liturgically similar, the major distinguishing characteristic between the two being that the former opens with a feast and the latter with a fast.

- Rosh HaShannah's mood is contemplative, yet celebratory, a new beginning for all of us.
- It is customary on Rosh HaShannah to offer visitors apples and honey and to bless those you meet with the phrase *L'shanah tovah u'm'tukah,* "To a year that will be good and sweet."
- It is also traditional to wear new items of clothing or to eat a fruit that is new to you so that you can recite the *Sheheheyanu* blessing (page 53) for the joy of having one more "first time" in your life.
- Each holiday has its own distinct melody, known as its *nusah.* Listen closely and you will hear how the flavor of the melodies in the Rosh HaShannah service differ from those of Yom Kippur, and how the mode of the *nusah* also changes from morning toward evening.

- Those who live near a lake, river, ocean, or *mikvah* (places appropriate for spiritual cleansing) will immerse themselves during the day before the sunset that signals the beginning of Yom Kippur.
- The spiritual tone of a fully practiced Yom Kippur is significantly different from that of Rosh HaShannah. No leather is worn on Yom Kippur, for who can truly contemplate the value of his own life while wrapped in the flesh of another? White clothes are worn because white is the color in Judaism symbolizing rebirth and the purity of intention you have worked to attain during the prior month of Elul and during Rosh HaShannah. This is also why the scroll covers are changed to white. Some will wear a white robe, called a *kittel,* which means "shroud," to more deeply embrace the end-of-life metaphors as all pray for another year of life. There is also a current of joy that flows through Yom Kippur, because we know that the Source of Life has designed us to return to the path of physical, emotional, and spiritual health. We know we are welcome back.
- On Yom Kippur we do not engage in lovemaking, eating, drinking, or washing. Except for children and anyone needing to take medication or to eat for health reasons, issues of the body are beside the point when matters of the soul take such serious precedence.
- The core Yom Kippur practice is to confront your-self during prayer by sincerely acknowledging errors and pledging to overcome them to the best of your

ability. Jews accept that the cataloguing, fine-tuning, and honorable cleaning up of mistakes, both individually and collectively, is a perpetual and essential spiritual process.

• As your life comes under the microscope of your consciousness, you may realize how essential it is to be a merciful audience to those asking for a *teshuvah* process with you.

2

Sukkot

Community and Meditation in Nature

After the hard work of *teshuvah*, the cycle of seasons allows some four days following Yom Kippur before you officially arrive at Sukkot, a soothing follow-up to the heartfelt soul work of the High Holy Days. No sooner does the shofar sound at the end of Yom Kippur than it is time to head for your yard, roof, or terrace to place the first nail of construction in an intentionally fragile ritual structure called a *sukkah*, modeled after the harvest huts used for shade in the fields of ancient Israel. During the High Holy Days, time outside in nature would, for the most part, be a distraction from the process, but on Sukkot it is the main point. Sitting outdoors in a *sukkah* creates a major mind-shift from the recent weeks of prayer inside a sturdy synagogue sanctuary.

The *sukkah* helps you to re-ground yourself after the soul-yearning of the High Holy Days. It is also a place of incubation, a safe space in which to get used to the expanded self you have ushered in through your spiritual practice of the previous year. After feeling so close to death on Yom Kippur, Sukkot, in a psycho-spiritual sense, is a return to the joy of being fully alive and in community. Indeed, in the festival prayer over the wine, Sukkot is called *z'man simhateynu*, "season of our happiness."

Sukkot, the plural form of its main ritual symbol, the *sukkah*, is a hands-on holiday. During Sukkot week, it is traditional to take your meals in the *sukkah*, to conduct rituals in your *sukkah*, study in it, and even sleep in it. It is quite wonderful to spend the night in the *sukkah*, under the stars, gazing in awe, and cuddling for love and warmth.

Sukkot emphasizes our interdependence with nature. The roof of a *sukkah* must be designed to provide partial shelter while letting the rain come in and the sun, moon, and stars shine through. One could see Sukkot as a weeklong meditation in nature, focused on appreciation of the greater housing within which we all dwell. Your house, my house, the harvest, the ecosystem, the cosmos—all combine to create a fully realized living system.

On Sukkot you are released from the intensity of self-scrutiny.
Leave fasting. Prepare for feasting.
Instead of knocking on the door to your heart,
begin tapping together your harvest home.

Whether it is for your inner child or an actual child,
while constructing the *sukkah*
you are building precious memories,
teaching and expressing Jewish values
about how teamwork builds spirit,
the importance of cherishing nature,
nurturing friendships,
feeling (w)holy in life.

This is a guided visualization to whet your Sukkot appetite. You can read it to yourself or read it out loud to your congregation, _havurah_ (a more intimate prayer or study community), or another group.

 Urge everyone to be seated in a comfortable position and begin to notice their breathing. (_Leader, take a few slow, audible breaths, so others present can join you._) Now do the following visualization.

RECIPE # 8
Especially for
Those Who
Work Indoors
All Day

 Imagine this is a day you went to work. On the way to work you noticed that the leaves on the trees were just beginning to change color. You noticed a light breeze, perhaps it is still blowing a bit out there. Once again you have made a plan in your heart to get back outside today, to leave the sturdy building that houses your day's efforts and, for at a least a few minutes, let the rays of soft autumn sunlight caress your face. Look, the sun's rays are crossing the room, catching dust in the air and pointing like an arrow toward your desk.

 Step away from your desk and walk down the hall, perhaps descending in the elevator, until you are again out in the sunshine. Walk along the sidewalk. Look, over there, there is a _sukkah_ along the side of a building at the top of that hill. (_Pause._) How curious. Begin to walk up the hill toward the _sukkah_. What does the sky look like just beyond the _sukkah_?

 You are getting closer; details of this _sukkah_ are emerging. No one seems to be around right now. This experience is yours alone. Slide your glance down the sides of the _sukkah_. Note how delicate it is, swaying slightly in the breeze. Someone has laced daisy-like flowers through the lattice sides.

Cross the threshold into the *sukkah*. Notice how the light changes as it is filtered by the green pine needles on the roof. The floor is a carpet of soft green grass. Your footsteps sink in luxuriously. *(Pause.)* There is a choice of a cushion, a chair, or a mat on the floor. Sit down in the spot that is just right for you.

Take a few more slow, deep breaths. Relax your hands, your back, lightly close your eyes. Feel the soft breeze on your face. *(Leader, allow a long pause.)* How do you feel?

Just sitting in the *sukkah* is considered a mitzvah, a sacred act of consciousness. Can you sense why? Let's take five or ten more minutes of being at peace in the *sukkah*. Ask any thoughts about the past or the future to wait outside; you are a human just being right now.

It is time to return to your place of work. Rise slowly; leave this tranquil space gently. You can return to it throughout the week of Sukkot.

Walk slowly back to the office continuing to feel the light breeze and the warm rays of sun on your face. What has changed? Will the work you return to be affected by the practice you just did?

If you are doing this visualization in a *sukkah*, you can say the simple blessing upon fulfilling the practice of sitting in the *sukkah*. *Baruḥ atah adonai eloheynu meleḥ ha olam, asher kid-shanu b'mitzvotav, v'tzivanu lay-shayv bah-soo-kah*, "to sit/reside in a *sukkah*." This tradition also includes blessing and eating a few ounces of something like cake, so that you have, indeed, partaken of the mitzvah of *sukkah* by eating in it.

The elegance of your house is irrelevant to Sukkot.
In this context of voluntary simplicity,
you will have guests over

> to your humble, sweetly decorated hut
> while also helping others fulfill the mitzvah
> of *hahnassat orhim*
> by accepting hospitality in theirs.

> For seven days you will dine in a fragile *sukkah,*
> with close family and friends,
> savoring the abundance and beauty of creation.

Rabbi David Wolfe-Blank taught: "A *sukkah* is like a filter."
And indeed, the *sukkah* filters

in	the rain and sun and shadow,
out	those whom you invite who don't choose to come,
in	those who do come to be joyful with you,
out	issues of wealth, fancy furniture, décor
in	pure hospitality and loving connections.

Who comes to your *sukkah* is not a matter of synagogue membership; it is by your invitation that guests will come. It is by the invitation of others that you will enjoy a week of spiritual socializing, sharing peaceful interludes in each other's *sukkot* for beautiful ritual and quality time in intimate community.

One of the great moments of Sukkot occurs after you make your list of who will be invited for which meals. Check to see if someone appears on the list whom you could not have invited last year. Is it someone with whom you have been doing *teshuvah,* perhaps for years? Is the wound now healed enough that you sense it is possible to bring this person back into your life as a regular member of your circle? When such a person arrives, you will notice that all the work you two have done to recover your relationship has indeed led you to know each other quite well; it is a moment full of blessing.

Many people think that the primary emphasis of Judaism is on Torah study. But knowledge is intended to inform life, not replace it. Marketing experts claim we are leaving the "information age" and entering the "relationship age." Jewish spiritual practice calls for a balance of the two—learning that infuses living, leading to wisdom and joy.

What follows is perhaps the simplest and most important of all the recipes.

RECIPE # 9
Who Is in the
Minyan of
Your Life?

A minyan, ten people, is the Jewish term for the minimum quorum for communal prayer or Torah reading. To give the blessing for healing, the *misheberah*, in synagogue, there must be at least ten who will say *ameyn*. Are there ten people who really care about you, and for whom you really care? Sukkot helps you bring the improved self you've worked on during the High Holy Days to your inner circle for a meaningful, well-supported life.

Create a list of the people who show up for you and for whom you intend to show up in life. While the synagogue community might or might not be your minyan of reference, here you will be reflecting upon your minyan of preference.

Contemplate your list.

Who is in the minyan of your life?
Who will show up for you when you
are hurting/sad, celebrating/hopeful?
For whom do you show up?

How would this world be different if every person had at least ten partners in caring? It is no accident that you can't put up a *sukkah* by yourself, that the moment comes when you need someone your height or taller to hold up that other side. By reaching out for that someone, perhaps by announcing after services that you have room for a guest in your *sukkah*, you begin to create that so often desired and so very elusive delight . . . community.

Judaism offers a principle called *hiddur* mitzvah. *Hiddur* means to "glorify" or "embroider," so the principle is to deliberately beautify a conscious, sacred act. Judaism is not usually an ascetic religion; it is more of an esthetic tradition. Making a ritual object more beautiful is part of this notion of embroidering a mitzvah.

RECIPE # 10
Beautifying Your *Sukkah*

You can add handmade decorations to the walls and ceiling of your *sukkah*, storing them over the years to develop an enjoyable collection. Suspending gourds and other newly harvested fruits and vegetables is traditional. Some people use fabric walls the white-sand color of bedouin tents, reminiscent of Abraham's time. Because I'm partial to a gypsy-like effect, we use multicolored silks. Colorful strings of lights are also increasingly popular. In the western United States, I notice, families are putting up chili-pepper-shaped lights. *Sukkah*-building kits can be ordered on the Internet, where you will also find guidelines for building a traditional *sukkah*.

Inside the *sukkah*, several symbols are taken in hand and shaken as part of an ancient blessing practice. The *lulav* is one of these items. It is a tree bough bouquet, composed of a palm branch bound with *aravot*, "willows," and *haddasim*, "myrtles." The other is a citron, a lemon-like fruit called an *etrog*, or, in Ashkenazi parlance, *esrog*. Creative touches might include acquiring or making a special box to set the *etrog* in to protect it. A *lulav* and *etrog* can be ordered over the Internet or purchased through synagogues and Jewish bookstores. Recently, while wandering through the Jewish quarter in Paris, we found them being sold right on the street from pushcarts, as is also done in Israel.

- Can you envision a *sukkah* you might create on your own? A spot with open access to the sky, a rectangular shape, and an open doorway and roof made of *skah*, natural branches that let in sun, rain, and starshine—these are the basic requirements.
- How many will you hope to seat? What materials appeal to you? With whom might you build it?

RECIPE # 11
The Mystery
Guest

One year, while studying the Sukkot themes of the fragility of life and concern for earth's ecosystems, I suggested to neighbors that we try a new tradition for Sukkot, that of inviting one mystery guest each night to dine in our shared *sukkah*. We thought this would be a way to make it fun for the children to learn and practice the mitzvah of *hahnassat orhim*, "the welcoming of guests."

- Draw lots to determine who gets to invite a mystery guest and on which night.

- The person who picks the mystery guest decorates a chair as a seat of honor for the guest. The decoration must be appropriate to the special nature of the guest.

For example, one night I arrived home to find that my children had decorated two welcome chairs with crunched-up soda cans, foil, newspapers, and bottles. Who could the guests be? They turned out to be the team who worked on the recycling truck that serviced our neighborhood. In this case one happened to be of Hispanic descent; the other from a recently arrived Polish family. Neither had ever been a guest in a Jewish home. After the regular *sukkah* rituals, we offered a toast in their honor and the children read an essay explaining why they saw the efforts of the recycling collectors as holy work.

In turn, the two men answered all the children's many questions about their lives and work, and we also answered lots of questions about Judaism. The clanking sound of the weekly arrival of the recycling truck became an invitation to visit with friends forever after.

- Place the *lulav* and *etrog* on a small table or chair in your *sukkah* and stand near it. You might look up through the roof of the *sukkah* and gaze at the sky. Also note the decorations, perhaps fresh and dried seasonal fruits have been strung and hung. Feel the abundance of this harvest time, how the earth keeps fruiting.

RECIPE # 12
Traditional Rituals with the *Lulav* and *Etrog*

- Face Jerusalem. Align yourself with all the generations who have participated in the *sukkah* experience. In your right hand, lift the *lulav* by the wicker handle in which it is usually set. The green ridge that runs down one side of the palm bow should face you. Shake it gently, then briskly. Experiment with letting your whole body enjoy the act of shaking this bough up and down, forward, to the right, behind, and to the left. Judaism is a very visceral religion. Go ahead—get into it!

Carola de Vries Robles, a founding leader of Makom Or Zarua, a Jewish spirituality program in Amsterdam, teaches that shaking the *lulav* is a practice of reorienting yourself in all directions, so you can reclaim your groundedness and centeredness in this new season of life. Doing this is essential after the High Holy Days, when the soul is strenuously reaching beyond the physical. The practice helps you to return to the reality of living in your body and the greater body of the environment.

- Pick up the *etrog* with your left hand, press it against your nose and inhale the sweet fragrance— a combination of perfume and lemon essence. Feel the glossy, bumpy rind. There is likely to be a bit of stem at the end; this is called the *pitom* (pronounced *pea-tome*) and is required for the fruit to be considered ritually ripe and usable.
- Now, with the *lulav* in your right hand, and the *etrog* (*pitom* facing down) in your left, bring your hands together. Reb Zalman teaches that one begins the shaking by bringing the *lulav* and *etrog* together toward your heart.

It is time for expressing the sense of blessing brought about by being in such a fragile place of contemplative beauty, to feel it in your heart, along with your role in maintaining creation. Gather for yourself a sense of receptivity to the abundance of blessings coming from every direction. If that is hard to attain, you might ask for blessings. Feel the Great Unfolding that is constantly evolving all around and through you. Sense what a miracle it is to be part of all this!

The traditional blessing for this moment is *Baru<u>h</u> atah adonai eloheynu mele<u>h</u> ha olam, asher kidshanu b'mitzvotav v'tzi-vanu* **al n'ti-lat lu-lav**, "upon lifting the lulav." The *Shehe<u>h</u>eyanu* blessing for seasonal changes is also recited at this time. In the Talmud we discover that this blessing has as its basis the term *z'man*, "time" or "season," which for our sages was an astrological concept. They believed that specific con-junctions of constellations were auspicious for the manifesta-tion of certain qualities—freedom at Passover, happiness at Shavuot, miracles at <u>H</u>anukkah, and so on. So this blessing is intended to magnify our awareness of just how precious it is to experience these times.

Open with the traditional *Baru<u>h</u> atah adonai eloheynu mele<u>h</u> ha olam* and then thank the Source of Life for *shehe-<u>h</u>eyanu*, giving us life, *v'kee'mahnu*, sustaining us, *v'higeeyahnu*, and bringing us to *la-z'man ha-zeh*—this very *z'man*, this very moment when we experience the blessings of this holy day.

- Having said the blessings, turn the palm of your left hand upward, so that the *pitom* of the *etrog*, where it is connected to the tree of its life, now points skyward.

• Now shake the *lulav* and *etrog* together, three times
in each direction; there are various customs for the
order in which you should do this. The most
common is to shake east, south, west, north, up,
and down. Another common version is: south,
north, east, up, down, west. Bring the energy of
each direction in toward you as you complete each
quadrant of shaking. Pause when you finish, and
notice any effect on your body and spirit. What is
new about your experience this year?

RECIPE # 13
Inviting
In the
Ancestors:
Traditional
and New
Approaches

In the Zohar, the major resource work for Jewish mystical
study, it is stated, "Seven shepherds descend from the Garden
of Eden and come to the *sukkah* as guests." From this verse,
the mystics built a practice of inviting the spirit of our ancestors into the *sukkah*. This practice is called *ushpizin*, "guests."

• Whose memory would you like to invoke? By
inviting in the memory of someone who was
important to you, whom you imagine those gathered would appreciate including in their experience, you and your guests will better come to know
each other. You can also invite deceased sages,
philosophers, writers, politicians, scientists, musi-
cians, and the like.

• Such an invitation might sound something like
this: "I'd like to invite in my aunts Ann, Miriam,
and Sylvia, who energized my life with uncondi-

tional support and a 'You go girl' attitude, and also my Uncle Jack, who so loved nature that he learned to sail at age seventy."

- Some couple the inviting of the ancestors with the singing of songs that include their names or stories. The seven traditional male guests are: Abraham, Isaac, Jacob, Joseph, Moses, Aaron, and David. Reb Menachem Azariah also included female figures, the seven prophetesses: Sarah, Miriam, Deborah, Hannah, Abigail, Huldah, and Esther. As you call them into your *sukkah*, feel their stories entering with them. Some rotate the order of the *ushpizin* by mentioning a different ancestral pair first on each day of Sukkot.

- The Talmud offers a rhyming Aramaic incantation for *ushpizin*. Recite this together for each pair as you welcome them in:

Tivu, tivu, ushpizin ee-lah-een.   Come in, come in, esteemed
                                      guests.

Tivu, tivu, ushpizin kaddishin.   Come in, come in, holy
                                      guests.

There is much ripe fertility symbolism in the Sukkot rituals. The long, quivering phallic palm section of the *lulav* speaks for itself, and the *etrog* might symbolize an ovary. Healthy community ritual is more than just rote action; it inspires a life of shared meaning. You might have those gathered in your *sukkah*:

RECIPE # 14
Engendered
Symbols

- Alone or in community, shake the *lulav* and reflect on the question: When I shake the tree of my life this year, what falls out?
- Hold the *etrog* tenderly in their hands, being careful not to knock off its umbilical stem; this is its memory of the mother tree of its life. Inhale her fragrance. Contemplate the questions: What have I harvested? And, during this season of my life, what new creative possibilities am I incubating?
- Allocating a set portion of time per speaker, invite a voluntary sharing of what came up for each person.

THE SHABBAT OF SUKKOT HAS A SPECIAL PRACTICE

The Shabbat of Sukkot is the traditional time to study the Book of *Kohelet*, Ecclesiastes, a part of Jewish wisdom literature. The intentionally frail *sukkah* structure is a reminder that any sense of permanence is illusion; it is the perfect structure in which to sit with elders who can guide friends and family in the contemplation of *Kohelet*'s honest, troubling, ultimate questions. The study of *Kohelet* creates an atmosphere of deep inquiry into the nature, transience, and meaning of life.

RECIPE # 15
Inviting
Wisdom

I have explored all that is done in this world of seemingly separate beings and selves, and behold—there is no profit in it. There is nothing but emptiness, impermanence, and the pursuit of control that arises when you do not see the truth. (*Kohelet* 1:14)

The translation above is Rabbi Rami Shapiro's, from his exquisite work, *The Way of Solomon: Finding Joy and Contentment in the Wisdom of Ecclesiastes*. *Kohelet* is but one of a number of Jewish texts that seem to have been written with the intent that they be studied as a meditation.

One way to do this is by reciting the words of the passages passionately, repetitively, letting them run through your soul stream. Then sit quietly, allowing multiple awarenesses to arise, be noticed, suffuse you, and then dissipate so that other "aha" moments will emerge.

To honor the sage within every elder in your family, you might distribute the verses from *Kohelet* in advance for them to comment on after the meditation time, or in place of it, depending on the comfort level of your guests. This creates a Shabbat Sukkot afternoon of honoring the elders in your family or congregational community.

3

Simhat Torah
The Practice of Scroll Reversal

The Sukkot season culminates in Simhat Torah, a day of rejoicing in the gift of the Torah because one whole year's cycle of reading it through has been completed. The last section of the scroll is read and the first verses from the very beginning of Genesis are chanted anew. On this day, some communities take to the streets, dancing with the Torah, often carrying flags with symbols of the twelve tribes on them, signifying our people's unity in diversity.

In parts of New York City, whole blocks are closed to traffic as people from throughout the Jewish community pour out of synagogue services to dance with and honor the experience of Torah. Perhaps you remember the media reports in the 1980s, when this happened in Moscow and Kiev for the first time since World War II. Despite warnings by the KGB (because practicing Judaism was prohibited throughout what was then called the Soviet Union), thousands danced with Torahs in the streets.

Where does the joy come from?

Would you consider taking the Torah into your arms?

Can you see yourself dancing with this inheritance?

RECIPE # 16
Unfurling
the Torah

Rabbi Zalman Schachter-Shalomi developed the following Simḥat Torah ritual:

- Have the entire community form a tight circle, one person deep. Then unroll the Torah around the circle, each person gingerly supporting his or her section by the edge of the scroll. Be very careful not to touch the words; the ink will lift off and gradually the Torah will become *pasul,* "unusable." Do not lay the Torah down on any surface to do this; it will tear. Only when every person holds a segment of parchment can the power of this ritual be felt and accomplished safely.

- Now, those who can read Torah, slip under the scroll. I suggest the Torah readers face each other in the center of the circle while all present recite the blessing for Torah study: *Baruḥ atah adonai eloheynu meleḥ ha olam, asher kidshanu b'mitzvotav la'asok b'divrei Torah,* "to be immersed/occupied with words of Torah." If you are doing this during a Simḥat Torah service, offer instead the blessings for having an *aliyah.*

- Next, the Torah readers turn and walk toward those who are holding the edges of the scroll. They all then explore the columns where they stand, and offer verses that strike them as possibly intended to be meaningful to the person they are facing. As the possibilities of the verses enter each person's heart, the light of Torah will become manifest in almost every face.

AS AUTUMN LEAVES

After Simhat Torah, it is time to take down your *sukkah*. While it is technically permissible to leave much of it, except for the roof slats, in place, few people do, because setting it up is so much a part of the spirit of the practice itself. Next year some fingers will be more nimble; those who once strung decorations will clamor to hold the tools and redevelop the design. Those who once held the tools, on the other hand, may now have stiffened fingers and ask another generation to lift the boughs to the roof.

As days darken sooner and the winter equinox calls, Hanukkah comes to bring many forms of light into the seasonal darkness.

4

Hanukkah

A Celebration of Holy _Hutzpah_

_Hanukkah derives from a root meaning both
education and dedication.
Is the study of history a spiritual practice?
What must we learn from history
if we are not to be condemned to live it over again?_

While technically a festival rather than a major holiday, Hanukkah contains within its history a fascinating number of dramatic developments in Jewish thought and culture. A deceptively simple celebration, called by the historian Josephus the "Festival of the Lights," Hanukkah poignantly connects spirituality, history, and politics.

The events Hanukkah celebrates occurred at a time when the soul of Judaism had almost been successfully snuffed out. A potentially lethal combination threatened the Jewish people: assimilation to Hellenism, the dominant culture in much of the world in 164 C.E., and the decision by the regional Persian ruler, King Antiochus V, to make the practice of Judaism illegal. Having a Jewish name had become illegal; observing Shabbat, keeping kosher, and circumcision were all punishable by death. Citizenship in Jerusalem required full apostasy under the new identity laws.

Irritated by intra-Jewish strife between the observant and the Antiochines (the government's name for those who became citizens), Antiochus decided to require public demonstrations of fidelity to the state's Hellenist version of religion, including the sacrifice and eating of pigs, sacred prostitution, and the placement of idols in the Temple in Jerusalem.

Some factions, most notably the pietist country Jews, who tended to be more religious and less assimilated than city dwellers, saw this loss of autonomy as a punishment from G*d for the Hellenizing of their fellow Jews. Many pietists chose to die as martyrs rather than give in. By proving their faith in this alternative way, the pietist leaders told their followers, they might be rewarded after this life. This was a new development in Judaism; the Torah does not offer a philosophy of life after death, resurrection, or immortality.

Between assimilation and martyrdom, the light was going out quickly. A creative intervention was needed. Someone had to act with *hutzpah klapei shamayah*, "religious audacity." In Mod'in, a village that exists to this day, the breakthrough came. A local priest, Mattathias, took Jewish empowerment to a new level by acting without divine instruction. Influenced by the analytical side of Hellenism, Mattathias applied what he had learned and declared that the divine right of kings to rule does not apply when an earthly king commands violations of the Torah.

Mattathias combined reason and Torah to make his next and most dramatic point. In Numbers 25:6–13, a man named

Phineas kills an Israelite man who is coupling with a Midianite woman to make of them an example that might stop a plague that had already killed twenty-four thousand Israelites. The Torah attributes the plague to intertribal sexuality. A venereal disease could very well have spread to the Israelites, one they had not encountered before and to which they, therefore, had no resistance. G*d's blessing for Phineas's intervention is given after the fact and, therefore, viewed by Mattathias as a blessing of human initiative. Citing this incident as precedent,

> Mattathias made a radical break with the past.
> He did not passively wait to see
> what would become of his people
> under the circumstances and
> did not accept the desperate situation as
> evidence of G*d's will.

Mattathias acted by striking at a roadside altar the government had set up to test the faith of apostates by seeing if they would sacrifice and eat pork; a government agent was on hand to kill those who would not comply. There, as a Jew capitulated, Mattathias stabbed the apostate, killed the king's agent, destroyed the altar, and fled to the hills to organize an alternative to assimilation or martyrdom, namely rebellion.

The usual Jewish practice has been to incorporate the best elements of the cultures with which we interact while maintaining the integrity of our way of life. This time, however, the assimilation had gone almost to the point of losing touch with our core being. It took some time and many martyrs for the relatively small Jewish population to realize just how corrupt their own leadership in the city had become and to grasp that they were being used for the empire's gain.

Mattathias's bold act inspired Jewish hopes for independence. A coalition of the pious, the pragmatic, and the assimilated fought back and won.
Without a prophet or a king to tell them what to do, the Jewish people discovered a new spiritual practice, activism.

It was, however, a difficult coalition to maintain. The pietists refused to fight on the Sabbath and so became martyrs. Later in the second century, the definition of martyrdom would be refined to apply only to those who were being forced at point of death to commit murder, idolatry, or illicit sexual acts such as incest or adultery. Much later still, Maimonides and other sages would seek to quell outbursts of martyrdom as misplaced piety, although some sages would still laud it. Enough of us listened, however, and our people survived.

Mattathias broke with the pietists when, again using the analytical skills he'd acquired from the Hellenists, he took a step toward the interpretation of a key point the Torah did not clarify: whether one should fight on Shabbat and live or refuse to fight on Shabbat and be killed. The Book of Lamentations says: "Turn the other cheek." Referencing a source from the core of Torah, Leviticus 18:5, Mattathias, however, decided it was better to "choose life."

It seemed like a miracle, the few against the many. In the year 164 B.C.E., Mattathias's son, Judah Maccabee, cut Jerusalem off from the Seleucid armies and negotiated a settlement that restored religious autonomy and authority over the Temple to the Jewish people.

The moment must have felt messianic to many of those involved, and, indeed, the expectation grew that related prophecies in the Book of Daniel were about to be fulfilled. Out of respect for the pietists in their coalition, the Maccabees waited several months past the turn of that year for divine intervention, but that which was written did not take place. A huge paradigm shift occurred as people began to accept that prophets would no longer guide them nor would miracles be the order of the day. Rather, human judgment would be required to continue the covenant, and people discovered they could act independently, without explicit guidance from G*d.

On the twenty-fifth of Kislev, three years to the day after the imposition of desecrating sacrifices within the Temple and without a sign from G*d or prophet, the Maccabees decided on their own authority to purify and rededicate the Temple. A new era was dawning.

THE SIGNIFICANCE OF THE MENORAH

The menorah is mentioned twenty-seven times in the Torah. Precise details of its construction are given when Moses is alone on the mountaintop, listening to G*d and seeing the Architect's vision (Exodus 25:31–40). The menorah, then, becomes a symbol of this listening and holding of the Light. It is shaped like a tree, for some a symbol of the burning bush where Moses first encountered G*d. The mystics say the light of the menorah is drawn from the _or ganuz_, the hidden residue of the original light of creation that was trapped by the _klippot_, "fragments" created by the big bang. By doing the mitzvah of lighting the menorah, you are reclaiming from primordial darkness some of the original *or ganuz* as energy for a mitzvah-centered life.

Torah is called a Tree of Life and is made of that original light filtered, condensed, formed into creation, and encoded in letters dancing with energy. The menorah symbolized the Tree of Life in the Garden of Eden. It is G*d as Torah, filtered through the prism of your soul, becoming each new way you discover how to live that manifests as holiness.

The original menorah had seven branches. The Hanukkah menorah has nine, to commemorate the Maccabees' eight-day festival for rededication of the temple, plus one extra branch for the *shamash*, a helper candle to ignite the others.

But what about the miracle of the cruse of oil lasting eight days? This and many other stories arose long after the event, entering the realm of sacred myth. The Hanukkah menorah, however, does recall miracles—that there was enough "oil," then and now, enough of the Jewish soul left after so much assimilation and trauma, to rededicate ourselves to the covenant of living as Jews. Even today a huge menorah engraved with scenes from Jewish history stands outside Israel's parliament, an enduring symbol of that dedication.

The Maccabees also decided on another act of holy *hutzpah*. Instead of retaining animal sacrifice as the focus of Temple dedication ceremonies, they took from the flame within their souls and made the main event the kindling of the menorah, its flames symbolic of the presence of G*d, through Torah, in our lives. Although less than one hundred years later this second Temple would fall, the flame of Judaism would not go out.

On the Roman arch of Titus,
commemorating the conquering of Jerusalem,
the Romans are shown carrying off the menorah in triumph.
The Romans didn't know that
the most precious part of all had been left behind,
carried in the soul-sparks of our people,
every one of us a branch
of a hidden menorah,
carrying the light.

RELIGION, POLITICS, AND THE SHADOW SIDE

The end of the Hanukkah story is not often discussed because it is very troubling. The Maccabean revolutionaries formed an ultranationalist leadership that would not tolerate diversity within the Jewish ranks. Their Jewish government killed intermarried Jews and those who combined practices from the larger culture with their Judaism.

Hanukkah's history ends with a sobering reminder
that every generation must deploy
its zealots cautiously.
The flame of the soul can cause a forest fire
of zealous devastation.

Hanukkah has one simple ritual, to be done "between sunset and when the last person is on the street," the lighting of a menorah, to be placed in the window.

RECIPE # 17
The Menorah
Meditation

- Increase the light by one more flame each of the eight nights, adding from the right, lighting from the left.
- After lighting, say the blessings that emphasize the Source of the miraculous, improbable survival of our path.

Baru<u>h</u> atah adonai eloheynu mele<u>h</u> ha olam, asher kidshanu b'mitzvotav v'tzivanu

l'hadlik ner shel <u>H</u>anukkah.   to light the <u>H</u>anukkah flame.

Baru<u>h</u> atah adonai eloheynu mele<u>h</u> ha olam,

sheh asah neesim l'avoteynu   that made miracles for our
[m] v'emoteynu [f]   ancestors

ba yamim ha-<u>h</u>eym baz'man   in those days and these
ha-zeh.   times.

On the first night the *Sehe<u>h</u>eyanu* (page 53) is also added to emphasize the unique qualities of this *z'man*, this time of miracles.

- Sit comfortably and simply observe the flames until they go out.
- If your mind strays from <u>H</u>anukkah, gently return your attention to observing the candle flames and release intruder thoughts; they will naturally arrive and need a gentle escort.

• On the last night, many people invite friends to
come over with their menorot. This practice fills a
room with light and contemplation, which may be
followed by a sharing of thoughts that have arisen
during this Hanukkah season.

Many generations have carefully passed the flame to you.
          Will your home be a temple for this inheritance?

5

Tu Bi-Shevat
Fruit for Thought

Until recently, Tu Bi-Shevat (the fifteenth of Shevat) was a little-known festival. Shevat is the lunar month that falls in most years around January, the month the Israelites decided which trees were of an age to be tithed a percentage of their fruit. Tithing is based on the spiritual principle that you really don't own the land or its fruits. What comes is a gift of creation, and in earlier times a percentage was given in gratitude to the Temple. Today, an equivalent monetary sum is given to support Jewish scholars, educational institutions, and reforestation efforts. This is also when we eat the fruits that have just come into season in Israel, especially the first crop, which is almonds, called by Israeli children the "queen of Tu Bi-Shevat."

The Kabbalists built additional meaning onto this holiday. Looking back at the story of Adam's eating from the Tree of Knowledge in the Garden of Eden, they developed a holistic ritual for the healing of consciousness called a Tu Bi-Shevat seder. This ritual involves the symbolic blessing and eating of four different types of fruit and drinking four different wines in a specific order, as well as reading four selections of mystical text that help to move participants up through the four levels of consciousness these symbols represent—the physical world, emotional levels of being, intellectual understanding, and beyond. It is an evening of progressive ritual intended to create a feeling of wholeness in those who partake. This is the kind of wholeness that existed in the Garden of Eden, before knowledge got in the way of the sweet state of simply being alive.

RECIPE # 18
A Mini–Tu Bi-Shevat Seder

- First, prepare a plate of fruits according to the Tu Bi-Shevat categories. There are variations in this practice, but the way I like to structure this is:

Assiyah Level: The physical world that masks what lies within.
Tree fruits with a rind or shell such as pistachios, walnuts, almonds, chestnuts.

Yetzirah Level: Your inner world of feelings, where seeds of new possibility reside.
Tree fruits with a soft exterior and seed within such as mango, peach, plum, tangerine, date.

Beriyah Level: Where utopian ideas and possibilities can emerge.
Totally edible fruits such as grapes, figs, raspberries.

Atzilut Level: Beyond the known or conceivable, where
there is only Being.
Some use only imagination here; others pass
essences around for a whiff—almond,
mango, peach. The palmelo, an Israeli form
of grapefruit grown in Jericho that naturally
smells as if it were marinated in an exotic
perfume, is perfect for this.

- Each course of the ritual begins by blessing a glass
of wine or grape juice—white, then pink, then
light red, then full red; winter, spring, summer, fall.
Bless, *Baruh atah adonai eloheynu meleh ha olam borei
p'ri ha gafen*, creator of the fruit of the vine.
- With each fruit, say the blessing *Baruh atah adonai
eloheynu meleh ha olam borei p'ri ha eytz*, "*Blessed is
Adonai, our G*d, governing principle [king] of the
world, creator of the fruit of the vine*," and then, in
silence, ever so slowly, savor the taste. After tasting
and sipping, invite family or friends to explore the
metaphorical significance of what you have tasted.

For example, the raspberry can be savored for *Atzilut*, the
dimension of emanation, where new ideas and possibilities
can emerge. How fascinating it is to see the tiny flavorful seg-
ments that make up its wholeness. This reminds me of how a
television image is formed from dots of color. Every aspect of
creation emerges as a whole from huge numbers of energized
atoms, like the apparently empty center of the raspberry,
which appear to be still and solid, and yet in reality are furiously cycling in and out of the room before I can even take my

next breath. May you be blessed, with each level of sharing, to increase the feeling of consuming awe that such ritual can engender.

Some years you might begin by asking each person to bring a particular fruit mentioned in the Torah, to research some scientific facts about it, or to share a story, song, or poem in which the fruit appears. The pomegranate, for example, appears in the Torah in the embroidery on the robe of Aaron, the high priest. This fruit is said to have 613 seeds, one for each type of mitzvah in the Torah. Here's a challenge question: What is the fruit Eve gives Adam to eat? (No, the obvious answer is not correct.) May it be that Tu Bi-Shevat takes you ever higher, by bringing you new perspectives from the Tree of Life.

6

Purim
Odd Lots of Spirit

I tell you, I saw them. They're all booing in the synagogue!
Can the new rabbi be that bad?

Did you hear what they said?
They're sending some nice Jewish girl to compete
in a beauty contest; the prize is a rich, powerful partner.
And it's an intermarriage! No kidding?
Must be a Reform temple. No, Conservative. Really?

She's hoping to replace a queen
deposed for refusing to appear naked?
Doesn't that imply that she will have to . . . ?
Guess she's not from a religious family.

You're sure it was a synagogue you passed?
Have you been drinking?
Oh, they were passing out free booze. You went in?
Full of royalty, you say. Kings, queens, princesses everywhere.

Big news? No I haven't heard.
Haman hung. Jewish queen appointed in Persia?
No wonder she married him.

Also a Jewish prime minister appointed,
some guy named Mordeḥai?
You must have heard wrong. Isn't Persia an Islamic country?
Zoroastrian? You made that up.
You especially liked the folks dressed like triangular pastries?
This is a joke, right?
No, it's a Jewish spiritual practice!

Costumes, clowning, satire, drunkenness, the improbable, and the impossible take center stage as safe space is created to shake out the terror generated by generations of capricious, horrible anti-Semitism. The celebration of Purim has to be the original humor therapy. It is an actual mitzvah to participate in this phenomenon, which is a passionate spiritual practice dedicated to keeping Jews sane. Here, anger is let out in play as the words of a novel that is hand-scribed on an actual scroll, *Megillat Esther*, are chanted aloud to the congregation. When reading the villain's name, the practice is to stamp, boo, hiss, and even bang and twirl a *gragger*, a grating noise-making instrument.

A people who prefers to be left alone to pursue peace and holiness has to respond to the frustrations of anti-Semitism somehow! In a life of eternal vigilance and attention to scruples, for those who do not have addictions it is even a mitzvah to get drunk, to, on this one day, savor the experience of blissful unawareness.

Scholars have enhanced the irony of Purim by finding that the events described in the scroll never really happened.

Difficult to date, but definitely written prior to 87 B.C.E., when it was translated into Greek, *Megillat Esther* appears to have been a romance novel or satire of the Persian Empire period, incorporating aspects of the Babylonian mythological goddess *Ishtar*, also known as *Astarte*, and the god *Marduk*. Notice how strikingly close these names are to those of the Purim heroine, Esther, and her cousin, Morde<u>h</u>ai (usually spelled Mordecai). Imagine that the communal reading and playful dramatization of this novel became so popular and cathartic an event that it entered Judaism as a spiritual practice!

There are five sacred books called *megillot:* Job, Ruth, Ecclesiastes, the Song of Songs, and Esther. But only Esther is maintained in the form of a traditional scroll. To listen to the *ganseh megillah*, the "entire story" of Esther, is more than an opportunity for venting and experiencing the healing that comes from clowning; there is yet another, deeper lesson embedded in Purim practice.

FOR WHAT WOULD YOU PUT YOUR LIFE AT RISK?

Megillat Esther speaks of the kind of capricious anti-Semitism that hurts and shocks because it is so unexpected and random. When the story opens, it has been a quiet time in Shushan, the capital of Persia, where the Jewish community is comparatively well accepted. So quiet that when Morde<u>h</u>ai uncovers a plot against the king's life, the king doesn't hesitate to accord him honors. Irritated by Morde<u>h</u>ai's refusal as a Jew to bow down to any human authority, the king's prime minister, Haman, decides to have all Jews killed. The king is distracted by other matters and signs off on Haman's plan. Too, it seems, he is not at all aware that he has married a Jewish woman.

Haman decides the date of the assault by drawing "lots," which is the meaning of the word *purim*.

The queen learns of Haman's evil plan and by courier discusses it with her cousin Mordehai. It is clear that only an edict signed by the king can reverse the terror that has been unleashed. Esther must speak to the king and convince him of this. But how? She has not been called to his side for three months. If she goes into his receiving hall and he does not signal his approval, the rule is that she must be put to death.

Queen Esther learns of a plot to kill all the Jews of Persia.
Only she has a chance to stop it.
But the king does not know she is Jewish.
She, herself, may be safe if she doesn't tell.
But the survival of her people depends on her taking action.
Will she risk her life to save them?
Would you?

RECIPE # 19
You Bet
Your Life

- Dress up and try on Esther's role. The Scroll of Esther invites *you* onto the stage of history. For what cause would you risk giving up your privilege, position, and lifestyle? For what would you risk your *life?*
- Try on the mask of Haman. Do you have him inside you, too? Or is the apathy of King Ahashverosh more your style? Better to discover and release these qualities in play than to act them out for real and destroy what it means to be a Jew.

Better to realize that such cruel qualities are present
in every human and too easily unleashed into society.
Playfully serious,
Purim prepares every child for quick turns in reality,
teaching very early that you cannot rely on government
to be concerned for your welfare.

The price of true freedom is eternal vigilance,
and Purim is a reminder that
you, the individual, are always on guard duty.
G*d is never overtly mentioned in *Megillat Esther*.
Maybe every face is the mask of G*d in the story called life.

Of the five *megillot*, *Megillat Esther* is unique because G*d does
not play a part in the story. This might be further documenta-
tion of the Jewish people's spiritual evolution away from the
G*d-as-parent model and their recognition that events may
have Mystery behind them and yet require human involvement if we are going to be of service in shaping creation. This
absence of G*d-by-name in the story also seems to facilitate
the permission participants feel to give full expression to the
playfulness of the holiday.

Our sages find G*d in *Megillat Esther* by pointing to
Deuteronomy 31:18. Listen to the sound of the Hebrew words:
Ah'noe'hi ha-stehr ahsteer, "I will hide my face on that day."
Can you hear how *ahsteer* sounds like *Esther?* So, on Purim,
G*d is also wearing a mask, that of Esther. Every day, you, a
stranger, your teacher, a partner, your neighbor, your enemy—
each has the potential to realize that she is in the Esther
position—able to unmask and bring a mitzvah-centered consciousness into difficult circumstances. The choice belongs to
the individual; the consequences belong to all.

THE EVER-EXPANDING PURIM TRADITIONS

In the story, Esther develops a plan to save her people that involves appearing before the king to invite him to a party. Since the queen is not allowed in the king's presence without prior invitation, she will be taking her life in her hands. Esther prays and fasts before she acts. She prepares a feast to which she also invites Haman. Haman arrives first and launches himself at her with the expectation of a sexual encounter. The king enters and catches Haman doing this to his beloved young queen. Esther uses this moment to reveal her Jewishness while denouncing Haman's plot, which would have required her to die along with all the other Jews in the kingdom. The king turns against Haman and adopts a plan presented by Esther to save her people.

- *Taanit Esther*, the Fast of Esther, is held on the day before Purim to express spiritual solidarity with her. Such a fast can be a powerful practice of preparation for experiencing the full drama of Purim.
- It is traditional to hold an afternoon feast to commemorate the fateful meal with which Esther seduced the king and denounced Haman's plot. The feasting and jesting of Purim are in memorable contrast to the Fast of Esther, the terror of both the plot and the realities of persecution, and the deprivation that has plagued many periods of Jewish history.
- In the spirit of rejoicing that ends the Purim tale, it is traditional to bring platters of cookies and sweets to neighbors and friends. This is called *mishloah manot*, "sending gifts." In various times, this practice has been accompanied by the ancient

Jewish version of trick or treat, with revelers coming costumed to the door, offering Purim antics, and receiving cakes. Nursing homes and other places that could be off the community map are important for *shlah manot* visits. *Matanot la-evyonim*, donations to food banks and other forums for feeding the poor, or direct cash donations to the poor, are also viewed as important Purim mitzvot.

CONFLICTING PRINCIPLES AT PLAY

Exercising power, overt and covert, is the name of the game in *Megillat Esther*. If one reads the story from a feminist perspective, one is inclined to applaud Esther's predecessor, Queen Vashti, who refused to appear naked before the king's courtiers. On the other hand, it is a titillating scene when Esther uses her gender, sexuality, and beauty to topple Haman. You'll have to read the *ganseh megillah* yourself to learn about the scheme she doesn't employ that had been proposed by her cousin Mordehai. It is, after all, her own life at risk. She knows the ways of the palace and her own talents far better than he. Is what Esther does ethical? The ethical dilemmas of Purim make for important study and encourage another Jewish practice, answering a question with another question.

Often we assume that the messages of the holidays are obvious. But moving from a message to true spiritual development requires a supportive context, that of conscious

RECIPE # 20
Purim
Questions

friendships, families, and communities. To benefit from Purim, it helps to begin by asking yourself questions, such as these:

- How can you bring more joy, humor, and release into your congregation's Purim celebration? When Haman's plot is foiled and Mordehai is appointed prime minister in his place, *Megillat Esther* says: "For the Jews there was *orah*, 'light'; *simhah*, 'happiness'; *sasson*, 'joy'; and *vee'kar*, 'cherishing.'" This verse is quoted in the Havdalah ceremony that ends Shabbat, adding the sentiment: *Keyn tee-h'yeh lanu*, "So may it be for us." We are a people who have long appreciated the healing value of humor. For example, there is the long tradition of the Purim Kiddush, which involves substituting bits of other prayers as you chant the usual festival prayer over the wine, as if you don't realize that's what you are doing. Go ahead. Experiment! Be playful!
- A gathering of female college students recently raised this question with me: Okay, so when is it appropriate to use your gender to gain advantage in this world? And when not?
- Are there times in your life when owning up to being Jewish requires courage and determination?
- How publicly do you wear your Jewishness? How comfortable is it to be a Jew where you live? When do you mask, unmask? What principles, values, and fears influence your decisions about this?
- What is it like to be Mordehai, serving as supporting male actor to a prominent woman, able to

mentor, recommend, and yet not control her decisions and movements? What are your thoughts on
the evolving conventions of gender and privilege?

- In the story, Ahashverosh shows his ultimate love
  for Esther by adopting her plan, which calls for his
  rescinding the decree and writing another retroac-
  tively that allows Jews throughout the kingdom to
  defend themselves. But since edicts went out on
  horseback in those days, he couldn't quickly call
  back the troops already out in the field killing
  every Jew.

- If you are not Jewish, and you are in a relationship
  with a Jewish person, how can you support your
  partner in exploring and securing the treasures and
  security of your partner's people? How will you help
  this precious legacy live through your children,
  your students, your art, your work?

- *Pur*, the root of *Purim*, refers to the lot that is
  drawn, the so-to-speak random roll-of-the-dice
  method which Haman uses to chose a date to
  launch his evil plan. Purim raises questions about
  how you, like Esther and Morde̲hai, can influence
  the odds of life for yourself and others. Has an
  opportunity to do this ever come up for you?
  When, how, and for what did or would you put
  your life at risk? This question merits discussion at
  the dinner table, with all generations present.
  Share from your life, about what you've learned
  and think about this. With your life, how can you
  influence the odds? Notice that the root letters
  of Purim, *pur*, also occur in the holiday name

Yom Kippur, a linguistic reminder that the impact of decisions past can very much influence how your lot will be cast in the years to come.

PURIM *SHPIELS*

To spoof authority, even the Highest, is a Purim tradition that does more than just allow us to let off steam, which is good in and of itself. In seminaries, yeshivas, schools, families, and congregations, it is customary for congregants to take turns spoofing Judaism and the characters of leadership past and present. Where this tradition is followed, a secondary gain occurs when a kernel of truth is revealed about the persons or practices being spoofed. A well-conceived *shpiel*, or spoof, provides precious insight, which can spark a rethinking of habitual patterns.

Often a person's hard edges mask a deep hurt, a sense of being misunderstood in the world, a place where the light is blocked although he may not realize it. Purim *shpiels* remove the masks our leaders wear. When humor is filled with affection and caring, and it is designed to remove the mask without inflicting more hurt, it is holy humor.

My first encounter with an adult-level Purim was in rabbinical school. Upon arriving for Purim services, I was quite shocked to see a bust of Rabbi Mordecai Kaplan, the denomination's founder, on top of the reader's table and the service leader bowing down to it. Idolatry!? Reconstructionism is creative and intellectual, but hardly idolatrous. Next, one of my favorite teachers got up and began to lead the morning prayers using Broadway show tunes! When we got to the Shema, out leapt a cluster of students dressed in top hats, tights, and scanty tails to sing:

One singular sensation. Every little step G*d takes.
One singular sensation. Every little move that She makes.

I'd grown up in a congregation where the Purim reading was recited in a monotone, the costume parade for children only. This was glorious, outrageous fun, and after some sixty hours a week of rabbinic studies, a delightful release and an important reminder not to worship the words or ideas of any one scholar or sage. Purim *shpiels* definitely top the charts during the month of Adar!

7

Passover
Learning the Exodus Process

Passover in Hebrew is *Pesa<u>h</u>*, from the verb *lifsoa<u>h</u>*, "to leap over," a word that reflects the very essence of this holiday. The Passover seder is the centerpiece of a sequence of practices designed to help us internalize an ancient and effective map for finding the *Ex-hodus*, "the way out" (Latin) of individual or collective oppression and making the leap to a better life.

The word *seder* translates as "order," and the seder itself is a carefully ordered, multisensory Exodus experience whose rituals embody levels of meaning that are available to people of all ages. Among the many potent seder practices is the display of a ritual plate filled with symbolic foods. From this plate we will taste bitter herbs as a reminder of the trauma of enslavement. Salt water will symbolize our ancestors' tears, and the parsley we dip into it will remind us that new growth often results from painful lessons learned. Throughout the seder and its festival meal we recline like Roman nobles, drinking four cups of wine with a blessing for each one to remind us that no human is the "lord" of life. We pour drops of wine from our cup to symbolize plagues brought upon our oppressors, and we send the children to find the matzah fragment known as the *afikomen* to symbolize the importance of their participation in uncovering hidden clues for healing the broken aspects of life. Finally, we open the front door to welcome the spirit of Elijah heralding *mashiah* consciousness, the potential for peaceful human coexistence.

The symbols, stories, and prayers embodied in the seder are meant to encourage questioning, exploration, and discussion of the principles inherent in Passover, especially the recollection of the struggle for liberation and the celebration of being fully free—physically, intellectually, and spiritually. While Rosh HaShannah emphasizes individual responsibility, Passover is about the birth of a nation based on shared, life-affirming values.

Some believe that the story of Passover is pure fiction. Was there ever really an Exodus? Were Jews ever enslaved in Egypt? Or were the Jewish people, as contemporary theories hold, simply a concatenation of oppressed peoples indigenous to what is roughly the greater modern Israel area of the Fertile Crescent? Were we immigrants who overthrew the existing leadership, or did we develop into a nation right where we started? While these questions are interesting to contemplate, the data is sparse and difficult to interpret; the answers lie in the past. The history, myth, and Exodus metaphor live on as memories strengthened by ritual, not so much to accurately recount events from the past as to place essential lessons in both individual and collective memory for the future. The seder, which is the most widely practiced of all Jewish rituals, is designed to ensure that everyone born into comfort will empathize with the pain of oppression, and that everyone born into oppression will know the hope and be inspired to take up the cause of redemption.

For those who are aware of the deep meanings of the rituals, the *seudah,* or meal itself, a festival feast enjoyed by empowered free people, is a complement to an equally delicious seder experience. Jews from every culture add their own flavors, melodies, liturgy, and ritual to the seder as a labor of love, in order to rebirth the Exodus as a foundational Jewish metaphor for remembering the importance of freedom and how to attain liberation year after year. The Haggadah (from the Hebrew verb, *l'hah'geed,* "to tell, or relate") appears in new interpretive editions every year.

I composed this visualization with my dear friend Laura Vidmar. It can be practiced in advance of Passover as a form of preparation or incorporated into the seder as part of the *maggid,* the telling-the-story section. Be sure to read the words slowly, with feeling, and honor all the pauses fully; they are very important elements. Depending on the time, you might invite sharing afterward.

RECIPE # 21
Crossing the
Red Sea

Allow your eyes to close. Inhale and exhale. Listen to the sound of your breath. Do you not hear the distant sound of an ancient sea? Listen to your breath from that part of your heart that remembers being there at the time of the Exodus from Egypt. Inhale and exhale as you hear the moving of the waters echoing in your innermost ear.

With your eyes still closed, look up, as if you were looking at the top of the pillar of cloud that is guiding us out of Egypt. Observe the form and color of the cloud and feel the hope and promise that it represents. Feel its pull on your soul drawing you toward freedom. Now allow your eyes to slide slowly down the length of the cloud, down and down, until you are gazing at the horizon. Notice the mass of people moving with you.

Feel yourself moving toward the sea in that ocean of Israelites. Are you leading children by the hand? Or are you a child yourself, moving quickly to keep up with the big people, wondering why there is no work to be done today? No bricks to be made, no taskmasters with whips.

Listen! In the distance you can hear the dim clatter of spears and shields, horses' hooves and the rumble of chariot wheels. The whinny of a horse, a muffled command barked by one of the charioteers or Egyptian captains. The rumbling of the chariots. Pharaoh's great army is coming behind us.

We are approaching the sea. Inhale the tangy, salty, watery smell of the sea. Feel the sand sift through your toes. Listen! Perhaps you can hear the bleating of sheep. And the children saying, "Mommy, Daddy, where are we going? What will happen to us?"

The familiar, the known, is behind. The sea lies ahead, and the wheels of Pharaoh's chariots are rumbling—coming closer. The wind is picking up. A strong wind from the East. A persistent, steady, seemingly purposeful wind. A wind that could change everything.

Your hair is flying and there are whitecaps on the sea. And then—Look! Moshe is holding out his hands—*my* G*d—the sea is beginning to split. It is a miracle! The sea has parted and there is a dry path before us. There is a huge, quivering wall of water on the left and a wall of water on the right.

What is in your heart at this moment? Will you rush into the sea with a trusting heart, running toward freedom, praising G*d . . . *or* . . . do you hang back—afraid of the unknown, afraid the walls of water will close and drown you? Are you afraid of being caught, afraid of change? (*Pause*) This is not an illusion.

Both choosing and being propelled by the crowd, almost numb with fear, curiosity, hope, and awe, you are moving forward into the sea. Even the children and animals fall eerily silent as you walk between the towering walls of water.

You can see the intense blue-green of the sea on either side. What do you see in the wall of water? Light filters through and casts dancing blue shadows on everyone.

Now we're halfway across. The walls of water on the left and right stretch as far as you can see in front and as far as you can see behind. Incredible! We are walking on dry land in the midst of the sea.

What an exhilarating sensation—*sheheheyanu*—to be alive at this time, to experience this. Even if we drown or Pharaoh's army overtakes us—*dayenu*. This would have been enough.

The chariots sound different now, their wheels scraping and groaning against the sea floor. You are beginning to hear the suggestion of a melody (*pause*) beckoning in the distance as you move toward the opposite shore. Could it be animals? No, voices. Singing!

Despite exhaustion, growing elation lightens your footsteps. Your heartbeat quickens. The pace of everyone increases, surges. Soon you are running, flying, eager to reach the opposite side.

A woman is singing. You join her. (*Being careful not to break the trance, begin softly singing* dayenu *or the biblical song of the sea,* Miha Moha. *Participants will tend to join in as they emerge from this visualization, and you can let the energy of the singing build and the seder continue.*)

THE PASSOVER SEQUENCE

Passover preparation begins the day after Purim. Reviewing stories, customs, and practices from Passovers past supports your annual reentry into Passover consciousness. It is a major task to reset the stage of your life in preparation for hosting a reenactment of the Exodus experience during the eight days of Passover. There are three major Passover practices in addition to the seder. Whether you engage in some or all of these, each element is valuable when practiced and understood through a spiritual lens.

- Throughout Passover it is a mitzvah to eat matzah instead of bread or other leavened products. Matzah is also called the "bread of affliction," because it was a low-cost, low-tech food for our enslaved ancestors and because, in their haste to flee, they didn't have time to allow it to rise. Throughout Jewish history, in times of religious oppression, having matzah in one's possession was often outlawed. Bringing matzah to eat at school or at work during Passover helps us to emphasize and exercise the principle of freedom of religion.
- *Bedikat ḥametz* is a ritual of checking for what I call anti-matzah, leavened foods categorized as *ḥametz,* which are removed from the *bayit katan,* "the small temple" of your home (and office) along with changing over to Kosher-for-Passover recipes, ingredients, pots, dishes, and utensils as a part of the scene change for staging this festival.
- You need not rush through Passover like a slave. The first and last two of its eight days are considered to be

like the Sabbath. One doesn't work or go to classes but chooses instead to further exercise freedom of religion by attending *sedarim* (pl.) and synagogue festival services, and by spending free, unpressured time with one's family. When you reserve time to savor Passover's rituals, ideals, and practices, your family and guests will experience the holiness, healing, and happiness of this transformative holiday.

PASSOVER PREPARATION

One year, my husband and I were out apartment-hunting in Manhattan, where the sorry condition of many of the places we saw finally induced him to ask why so many obviously middle-class people lived in such undignified messes. The real estate agent answered instantly: "They don't really live here. They're too busy working." Passover is the antidote to this kind of life. The emphasis is on your home as sacred space, your kitchen and table are the altar, and the condition of your space reveals your inner temple.

Sensitive to the disorder that naturally occurs in all spaces, even the most sacred, Passover establishes a process for setting things right, for redirecting your attention to your home, however temporary it may be.

Before Passover begins, walk through your living space. Open each cabinet in the kitchen and bath. Lift the bed skirts, open the closet doors, look in the refrigerator. Notice what is inside.

RECIPE # 22
Closet Space

Technically you are looking for _hametz_, foods made with leavening or those prepared before the place was _kashered_, "made kosher," for Passover. This practice helps to place us in the Passover mind-set—leaving Egypt, having no time to let the dough rise, ending up with matzah, more a cracker than a bread; fleeing, losing familiar home and hearth, having to set up a household from scratch on the desert road to freedom. Passover practice connects our daily lives with the Exodus experience, all the way down to the details of the kitchen. We are remembering how hard it has been to survive for so long, lest we take our survival for granted.

Stay with me, even more is happening here than meets the eye.

Contemplate what you see. A box of cereal, a loaf of bread, a cupcake. That's the obvious _hametz_; let's also look for other kinds: caffeine, chocolate, work, shopping, maybe bigger addictions. What did you find?

Look deeply within;
Passover is a weeklong exodus
from your patterns of consumption.

Can you empty the cabinets and
reset the stage of your life?

You have a support group
around the Passover table.

Who has time for all this? It can be a sobering exercise to open up all your cabinets, contemplate what's within, and clean it all out. What is really going on that could have resulted in the evolution and retention of such a labor-intensive practice?

Since your home is a temple for your personal life, this Passover practice is a reminder to be sure that what you have on-site meets your criteria for what is sacred. It is important to do this with friends, partners, and children.

You may find, as I have, that hidden within the ancient ritual of *bedikat hametz* is a secret spiritual benefit that also strips away any rationalization for the martyrdom of cleaning alone. This became clear some years back when my sons came home from school claiming they'd been instructed to search the house for *hametz* the most traditional way, with a candle, a feather, and a spoon. Despite my initial objections that this was archaic nonsense, we gave it a try.

It was, however, the addition of another very basic Passover practice, asking questions, that brought the experience to life when first I asked, "Why do we need a candle to look for *hametz*?"

They had a ready answer. "Because we have to look everywhere, even in the dark corners."

"Why everywhere? Does it really matter if we miss a crumb?" Again, they were ready for me.

"Mom, *hametz* is what Grandma Libby calls *shmutz*. It's under the beds, in the corners. You can't get freedom if there's *shmutz* around. This is about freedom!"

We were in the den. I'm thinking: Who was it who imagined that housekeeping was about freedom? And then the younger one, Mark, pipes up with, "Mom, you know how you describe people's saying mean things as a way of 'getting *shmutz* all over your soul?'"

"Yes, so?"

"Maybe that's really the *shmutz* that's hiding in the house. Like all the times I took the remote control away from Adam or punched him and called him names."

The little guy had really offered something of substance to reflect on. Pushing the idea a little further, I noted, "So, that's a great explanation of what the real *ḥametz* is that we're looking for. Let's try it in each room." Then the next question came to me: "Why do we have the feather?"

The older one put it perfectly, acute impatience in his voice at the idea that I'd even had to ask. "*Mom*, you wouldn't want to use a pitch fork, would you—not on our feelings?"

So we went from room to room, reflecting on the aspects of *shmutz* that had gotten onto our relationships in the home, collecting lint and crumbs, bobby pins and a missing sock—representative of our family *ḥametz*. Then there was the question of the spoon.

"Mom, why the spoon? We already know it symbolizes the altar for *korban Pesaḥ* (the lamb sacrificed by the Israelites after their successful escape from Egypt), but what did sacrifice mean in those days? Why do we take the *ḥametz* and burn it up in the spoon?"

How do you explain *resistance* to children? That people don't change so easily. All we can do is collect our little piles of *shmutz*, lay them on the altar of our intentions, and focus the light of hope and love in such a way that some of it will burn away. Ancient rather than archaic, the ritual turned out to be designed to help mistakes decay into personal fossil fuel, which then becomes a source of energy for living with greater consciousness.

Many families include an egg in a bowl of salt water among the ritual foods at their seder to symbolize birth and the breaking of the waters that released the Israelites from *Mitzrayim*, Egypt. *Mitzrayim*, as I've already mentioned, comes from the root *maytzar*, which is also the word meaning "birth canal," "strait," or "narrow place." A nation is being born.

A Passover preparation practice of the Jewish mystics that you might consider adopting is to expand the Exodus process by rebirthing yourself through immersion in a *mikvah*, a body of water that is a "gathering" of living waters. Traditionally, this is done in a lake, a river, an ocean, or in an indoor pool created for this purpose. You might submerge several times in this symbolic cosmic womb, contemplating the ways you wish for yourself, our people, and all people, to be more fully free; shaking off any personal *hametz*—ways you sabotage your own freedom—and then emerging fully open to the power of Passover week. The blessing for immersing in the *mikvah* is: *Baruḥ atah adonai eloheynu meleḥ ha olam, asher kidshanu b'mitzvotav v'tzivanu al ha t'vee-lah*, "regarding the immersion." Or some of us might prefer a more feminine *mikvah* blessing, so one I've developed with Rabbi Judy Kummer is based on the root of one of the many names for G*d, *Ha-Raḥaman*, the Womb-like or Compassionate One: *Nevarekh et ha-raḥ'mana eyn ha-olam asher kidshatnu bi-t'veelah b'mayyim ḥayyim*, Let us bless the Womb-like Source of the Cosmos, making us holy through immersion in living waters.

RECIPE # 23
The Egg, Mikvah, and Rebirth

RECIPE # 24
A Spiritual
Menu for
Your Passover
Seder

Every Haggadah begins with an identical listing of the traditional sequence of the seder rituals. Rabbi David Wolfe-Blank, of blessed memory, would often mail his students spiritual annotations for Jewish prayer, including the Haggadah. Developed in honor of his memory, this recipe will take you on a spiritual tour of the seder. I hope you will consider developing your *own* menu of Passover spirituality, or try creating your own annotated Haggadah. Preset Hebrew for the Haggadah (as well as the siddur and Torah) is widely available via Hebrew/English word processing programs that work much like Word and Word Perfect. These programs can be found at some Jewish bookstores and on websites such as Davka.com, Jewishsoftware.com, Levsoftware.com, SolomonsTreasureChest.com, and Nisus-soft.com.

A SPIRITUAL PASSOVER SEDER MENU

Kadaysh
Chanting the Kiddush over the Wine
Through this wine may we be strengthened for our journey into memory, into the flow of time where mikra kodesh, *"holiness happens."*

Raise the brimming kiddush, "holiness," cup of red wine. Wine is the symbol of *gevurah*, "strength," and brimming over "vitality," the abundance mind-set that it takes to commit and to let go of what you have in anticipation of a better future.

Urhatz
Washing the hands
May loving-kindness wash through me during this experience with family and friends.

This handwashing is a moment of ritual purification. Water is our symbol for *ḥesed*, overflowing loving-kindness. You are the high priest for your seder and so you might guide those present to immerse their hands and then lift up their intentions for words of loving-kindness to fill this seder time together.

Karpas
Eating a bit of green vegetable

May the memory of tears past and any tears to come, moisten my heart that it be a fertile place for courage and love to flourish.

A green vegetable is dipped in salt water or vinegar, symbolizing tears. This is an appetizer of what is to come, new green shoots of life after deadening enslavements of body, mind, and spirit.

Yaḥatz
Breaking the middle matzah

I hold this matzah in front of my heart and pause to recall brokenness from the year gone by. As the sea parted for the Israelites, I break this matzah to let in the light of healing for myself and those of all nations.

Half will be hidden; this is the bread of unawareness. What will it take to experience redemption? Do you know? Even if not, the meal can't be finished without taking a taste and chewing on what the ingredients of redemption might be!

Maggid
Telling the Exodus story

(This is an interpretative translation of a Ḥasidic meditation. *Sheḥinah* is a feminine Hebrew noun for the experience of G*d as the capacity for presence, intimacy, and change. G*d as *meleḥ* or *kadosh baruḥ hu* refers to structure of creation, law, letters of Torah; *Sheḥinah* is the energy and spirit that flows through it all.)

Here I am, prepared and invited to sustain the sacred act of telling the story of the Exodus from Egypt, for the sake of realizing the illusion of any separateness of Oneness of the Holy One, Blessed Be with Sheḥinah, *so hidden and secret yet present through us.*

After the invocation to the left, become the story as it is told. Feel yourself as Moses appearing before Pharaoh; taste the bitterness of slavery; imagine the plagues all around you. Take the opportunity before you. Trust, flee, leave Egypt! Despite feeling that you will die, cross the sea. Rejoice! Feel the surging current of creation alive, pouring through you.

Ra*htz*ah
Washing the hands before eating
(The following verse is from a prayer composed by Rabbi Judy Kummer.)

"I lift up my hands in thanks for Your blessing."

No blessing accompanied the first washing. Now, the meal is about to begin, and we wash again, lifting up our hands with holy intentions, blessing the Source of all there is.

Motzi
Blessing before eating a meal with a bread substance in it
May this bread renew my connection to the process of creating life from dust.

Lifting up the two whole and one half matzah pieces, bless the creative process of nourishment coaxed from what once was simply earth.

Matzah
Blessing over the three sheets of unleavened bread, breaking one to hide for later, eating the matzah
When I have nothing left to draw on, matzah teaches me to trust and go on.

Two of the matzah sheets are a reminder of the double portion that came on Shabbat in the wilderness. Hurrying toward freedom is a worthy goal, and one half sheet more reminds you to hold on; the rest is coming.

Maror
Blessing bitter herbs; eating some
Bitterness comes into every life. May I learn enough not to pass this way again.

Bitter lettuce heart or horseradish is eaten; just enough to raise the memory of bitter times. You bless the Source of this pungent reminder that life has ebbs and flows. This too shall pass.

Kore*h*
A matzah sandwich is made with bitter herbs and sweet apple/date/nut/wine mixture called *h*aroset
(inspired by a song by Naomi Shemer)

May I learn equanimity, to take life as it comes, to bless the bitter with the sweet.

Reclining to one side, not enslaved to time nor any pharaoh, there is no need to bolt down your food, to run off to work. Pause, taste the spice of life.

Shul<u>h</u>an Aru<u>h</u>
Festival table arrayed with the delicious Passover meal

May the love added to this food during its preparation fill me so I am pregnant with celebration, bursting with passion for freedom. May all who hunger come and eat.

It is a mitzvah to contribute to the meal with foods created by your own hands. May you find this holy effort joyful to both give and receive. Feasting in freedom is so precious; no generation dare take it for granted.

Tzafun
Finding and eating the matzah half called the *afikomen*

Around the table may be those who almost lost Judaism as a spiritual path. (Pass pieces of the afikomen around for those who so identify, so they can take a piece of the whole.) May we all be blessed to add our questions and answers to Judaism as an evolving tradition.

The young people now search for the hidden *afikomen*, sometimes helped by family. Some reward only the child who finds it. When sending them on a search, perhaps offer a reward for all if they work together as a team.

No matter which part of the family we come from—religious, unaffiliated Zionist, secular humanist—we are one people, and we need to remember how to work together.

Bare<u>h</u>
Blessings after the meal
(inspired by the Talmud, Cantor Jack Kessler, and Rabbi Shefa Gold)

Bri<u>h</u> ra<u>h</u>amana malka d'alma marei d'hai pita. *Blessings upon the Compassionate One, Owner of this morsel. You are the Source of Life for all that is and Your blessing flows through me.*

It is so much easier to feel the flow of blessings after eating. In the Talmud (Bera<u>h</u>ot 50b) the sages note that the first verse of the traditional blessing after the meal reads: "*in* Whose goodness we live." The sages say it is important to note that it does not say "*through* Whose goodness we live." Perhaps this is to remind us that the Source of Life flows through us. The verse says *we*, not *I*, for it is the collective behavior of humanity that defines the quality of life for most living beings.

Hallel

Psalms and songs of celebration

I am filled with awareness of the gift of being alive at this time, in this place, and through the uniqueness that is me, my people, and our spiritual path.

Nirtzah

Concluding the seder

On this holy night, guide us, Your seedlings, so that next year in Jerusalem there will be _____ [invite those present to fill in here with their hopes]. *Lift your cup to the Mysterious, Unnamable, Limitless Awesomeness and say, "Next Year in Jerusalem!"*

The Kabbalists call these psalms "vessels of grace." The mystical commentary *Sefat Emet* suggests that when we are praising the Source of All, our blessing is taking place in the three vessels in which creation manifests: time, place, and soul.

At Sinai the Israelites declared: *Naaseh v'nishmah,* "We will do and we will listen." Logical order seems reversed in this verse. It is the seder that illustrates what the verse can mean. Through the *doing* of ritual, we *listen* in on the wisdom of teachers, ancestors, family, friends, and the Source of Life. Through the seder comes new guidance for the human journey toward freedom, year after year.

EXPANDING YOUR SEDER CREATIVITY

Many people collect various editions of the Haggadah for study and to distribute among their guests so that they can interject new music, liturgy, translations, and commentary during the seder. It is also traditional to encourage guests to bring poetry, songs, pertinent questions, and commentary to share during specific parts of the seder. Following are two recipes that work well when you invite participation from seder guests.

RECIPE # 25

What Would You Take with You?

A World War II survivor once showed me the little stack of photos showing the faces of her loved ones that she'd clipped out of larger pictures and sewn into the leg of her pants just before she fled her home in Poland.

- As a topic of conversation for your seder table, you might ask those present to contemplate and then discuss the following question: "What would you choose if you had to flee and all that you could take with you would have to fit in your dinner napkin?"
- You might expand the question by saying: "You can take two kinds of things with you—material things and the qualities of yourself that you believe will be your best assets for this part of your journey. What will you take?"
- Consider adopting the Sephardi custom of having your guests place their napkins over their shoulders for a symbolic Exodus walk around the table, or around the outside of the house. This can be done while chanting.
- Similarly, some families also have each child walk around the table carrying his/her napkin, stopping at each adult, who asks the child: "Who are you, what are you carrying, and where are you going?" To which the child answers with his/her Hebrew name, "I am _____ *bat/ben* (son/daughter of) _____ and _____. I am leaving slavery in order to be free. I am carrying (mentions what s/he has decided to take along), and I'm bound for the Holy Land." The adult then responds, "_____ *bat/ben* _____ may your journey be blessed!"

RECIPE # 26
Diluting Your
Plagues

For a more mature audience (including teens), you might try this practice just before the recounting-of-the-plagues portion of the seder.

- Each person turns to the person beside him, or the person sitting opposite.
- Each has a cup of red wine, and between them is one bowl of clear water.
- Take turns sharing something that is plaguing your awareness, something that has been a plague at some point in your life, either personally or in society at large. (This is not a cult. No one is required to reveal personal issues unless it feels right and the space feels safe enough to do this.)
- For each plague shared, pour a drop of your wine into the water. Water symbolizes the divine nature of overflowing loving-kindness.
- Take turns until the leader calls time, or until each person feels emptied of her plagues.
- Offer a blessing for the pain of these plagues to be diluted by the process of sharing, for a time when, like the Passover experience, the pain can be remembered as part of the journey and not become the only story in a long life.
- You might conclude with the observation that, in the family/community that has gathered, there are many who would gladly mentor and listen at a deeper level at a future time. If you are doing this in community, you might provide a contact

number for those trained in chaplaincy or who are available for spiritual mentoring.

ADDITIONAL PRACTICES

- The night before Passover, firstborn sons either fast, *taanit be_hor*, or attend a study session known as a *siyyum*, "summary," offered by someone who has just completed a page-by-page study of a major sacred text. This is done in commemoration of the traumatic passage in Exodus that describes an angel of death killing the Egyptians' firstborn, human and beast, in order to terrify the pharaoh into letting our people go free. This practice honors both the privilege of having been "passed over" for this terrible fate and the sadness engendered by the terrible traumas inherent in the struggle for liberation.

- On the first two days, two Torahs will be taken out for special readings at festival services and all can join in singing the joyous series of festival psalms known as the *Hallel*, "praise." A partial *Hallel* is chanted on the last two days, because the seventh day commemorates the parting of the Red Sea and so our joy at becoming free is tempered by sad awareness of the deaths of so many Egyptian soldiers.

- Mystics use round *shmurah*, "watched" matzah, for the plate of three matzot (pl.) used at the seder to represent the Jewish community, which is composed by tradition of priests *(cohanim)*, Levites, and regular Israelites. *Shmurah* matzah is handmade and baked on huge, flat oven stones. Those who prepare it make sure that the simple ingredients are mixed, the dough rolled out, perforated, and baked in no longer than eighteen minutes, the length of time after which fermentation begins. (The number *eighteen* in Jewish mysticism stands for "life.") Workers carry the rolled-out sheets of matzah to the ovens draped over wooden staves while chanting to keep their intention focused on *l'shem*, "for the sake of" mitzvah matzah.

• Passover foods require special recipes that adjust for the absence of leavening. The usual respect shown for the sanctity of life reflected in *kashrut*, "kosher" cooking by separating milk—a symbol of nurturance—from meat, which involves slaughter, is maintained. There are regional customs about which foods are permissible on Passover. Sephardim (Jews from Yemen, Spain, Italy, and so on) generally allow rice and beans, a food category termed *kitniot*, whereas Ashkenazim (those of Eastern European descent) do not, unless they are committed vegetarians.

• Some also hold a seder on the last night. Called *Seudat HaMashiah*, the Feast of the Messiah, it is replete with a liturgy of hope and joy that emphasizes the evolution of life far beyond what we now have.

• The Chernobyl Rebbe, of blessed memory, kept a record of occurrences in his personal life that he considered miraculous. He would share excerpts from these journal entries at the seder. Imagine, if we each did this, how much more fully we might appreciate the gifts that come with freedom!

8

Shavuot
Renewing Vision

Imagine:

Suddenly you are free to choose,
for yourself alone,
every rule and regulation.

Shavuot, meaning "weeks," is celebrated seven weeks after
the Exodus, and it is, by the conventions of tradition, the day
the urgently needed, civilization-shaping guidance known as
Torah was received at Sinai. The sages called this holiday
z'man mattan Torah, "the time of the giving of Torah." At this
time one either makes a pilgrimage to Israel or prepares to
attend services at home with a view toward reexperiencing
the giving of Torah at Sinai.

PREPARING FOR SINAI

Mystics emphasize the importance of preparing for Shavuot.
They point out that leaving Egypt does not deliver the

Israelites directly into the Promised Land of which they'd dreamed. Have you ever experienced a gleeful rush of joy after facing your fears and taking the leap necessary to get yourself out of a place of oppression? If you have, you'll also know that at some point reality sets in; you have entered new territory. It's time to slow down and figure out how to live in this new context. So many of the structures that held your world together are things of the past. This is characteristic of many experiences— for example war, divorce, emigrating to a new country, giving up a long-held career. Many of us who look back on these wilderness experiences realize that they were times for retooling ourselves in hope of attaining a better life. Our mystics realized that these times do not have to be characterized by complete chaos; we can use them to work on ourselves quite consciously.

Following Passover's leap into a new life, the forty-nine days leading up to Shavuot can be viewed as the Israelites' pilgrimage toward awareness; awareness that their mixed multitude of fleeing slaves is becoming a people, and readiness to find a better code of collective conduct than they suffered under in Egypt. Cognizant that each person will be inspired quite differently by the same words of Torah, teachers of Jewish mysticism emphasize the importance of Jewish methods of advanced awareness training during the seven weeks that lead to Shavuot. There are four major stages of Shavuot preparation:

- **_Omer_ practice.** Once the Temple was up and running in Jerusalem, the days from the Exodus to arriving at Sinai came to include worship rituals such as waving sheaves and making offerings of refined grain in a measure called an _omer._ In time the measure gave its name to the ritual through which these offerings were made. In place of waving an offering of wheat at the Temple in Jerusalem, Jewish mystics not only say a blessing for each day of the *Omer* but also engage in a daily self-study of personal polarities and practice conceiving of them in balance with one another.

- **Study of *Megillat Ruth*.** The story of Ruth, Boaz, and Naomi emphasizes three key points: that being Jewish is not a matter of genetics, it is a personal choice; that our people is made up of individuals from virtually every civilization; and that one's primary ethical obligation is to care for the poor, orphans, and those who are widowed.

- **Lag b'Omer.** A somber mood prevails during the *Omer*. No weddings or festive preparations are made until the *yahrzeit* of a renowned Jewish mystic, Shimon bar Yoḥai, is observed on Day 33 of the *Omer*, when, for some, festivities, shaving, and haircuts are resumed.

- ***Tikkun Leyl Shavuot.*** On *erev* Shavuot, the "eve" of the holy day, the mystics would "pull an all-nighter," as we said in college, by holding a communal, nightlong Torah study session. The Sinai experience was a time of waiting for revelation. By tradition, on Shavuot our people and all Jewish souls are camping anew at the base of the mountain. Also, as on other major holidays, *mikvah* immersion prior to sunset on the day Shavuot begins is observed as a process of spiritual cleansing after the long journey.

OMER PRACTICE

In addition to its biblical association with the giving of the Torah, Shavuot is also called the _hag habikurim_, "season of first fruits," the beginning of one of several harvest times in the Middle East, and specifically the time when offerings of grain were made to the Temple. According to the Talmud, one-tenth of the grain was mixed with oil and frankincense and burned to create a _rey'ah hah'nee-ho'ah_, "a pleasing aroma." This was intended as a sort of smoke signal to G*d, upon whom the ancients apparently projected a love of the smell of good barbecue.

Since the destruction of the Temple, however, the memory of this system is preserved by announcing at synagogue services which day of the _Omer_ it is, and by saying a blessing at home to account for each day of the _Omer_. When our mystics looked into this with their interpretive lens, they found a new form of offering: your "self." No, not putting yourself physically on an altar; rather, they offer an _Omer_ counting practice to help you "wave" aside a bit of resistance in order to get some aspect of yourself into better shape. Receiving Torah at the end of the _Omer_ process will be far more profound if your vessel of self is well prepared.

Just as the Torah is described as a Tree of Life,
the Jewish mystics have identified
a Tree of Life within _you_.

Since the Shavuot Torah passages
are going to go through _your_ consciousness,
your inner Tree of Life must be readied.

Each of the forty-nine days of *Omer,* and each of the seven weeks that comprise those days, is assigned one of the seven qualities described below. These qualities are considered branches of the Tree of Life, which is a metaphor for Torah as a manifestation of G*d consciousness.

Until this point, I have resisted giving an extensive introduction to Kabbalah. I do not approve of Kabbalah being studied independent of the many primary forms of Jewish spiritual practice. The Kabbalists themselves understood that a solid life of integrated Jewish practice is the necessary platform for their findings, yet, to this day I regularly encounter people who treat these as exotic practices for entertainment or imagined magical value. Absolutely not. Authentic mystical work is intended to bring you to a higher level of consciousness within the context of a grounding community of reference and regular Jewish practice. It is easy to get off base with the advanced forms of these practices and become a rogue and dangerously charged person. But it is also possible to become spiritually enhanced and of greater service to humanity through this work. The balanced practice of the basic forms of Judaism will help you become a safe vessel for the delight and importance of these mystical methods.

You can safely start by taking some inspiration from the Kabbalists' model for the *sephirot,* branches or rungs of the Tree of Life, which they perceive as having grown from the first spark of the big bang and having rapidly evolved into the qualities known as *sephirot* and then condensed into matter, and hence into individuals like yourself. Reflecting their holographic understanding of the universe, the Kabbalists see these qualities flowing through you as a microcosm of the macrocosm, All of Being. And they are wise enough to sense that what we experience as All of Being is probably only a fraction of what is, that beyond our universe there is likely another reality, where the full mystery of whatever G*d might be is expressed.

Sephirah means "sapphire" or "brilliance." Each *sephirah* has acquired a cluster of related meanings over time. The ten *sephirot* flow in a particular sequence and are often superimposed over a graphic of the human form set inside of a Star of David. Seven are used in the *Omer* counting practice. Three more—complete understanding, complete wisdom, and enlightenment—are considered higher-level functions, which, the mystics say, we can only work our way up to and then "suck" like a baby in the hope that some of the greater consciousness will accrue to us.

For the sake of giving you a good yet brief start, a simple explanation for some of the qualities of each lower *sephirah* is offered below.

The seven lower *sephirot* are:

Hesed: Overflowing loving-kindness, unconditional love, flow without boundaries.

Gevurah: Strength, boundaries, restraint, discipline, limits.

Tiferet: Beauty, harmonious cooperation between opposing forces, compassion.

Netzah: Endurance, ambition, drive, focus, ability to sustain.

Hod: Containment, incubation, refining, wrapping the present, quality development.

Yesod: Foundation—conducting, transmitting, sending it toward its audience.

Mal<u>h</u>ut: Here you are ready, as Reb Zalman teaches, to press "Enter," to dissolve your focused efforts, to let go and experience, to be present to what will become of your efforts in the real world.

Studying the *sephirot* is a way of getting in touch with yourself so that when you are living your life and studying Torah, you are doing it as an aware individual. Every attribute of human behavior is within you, and whether any one exists as a developed asset or as a deficit is often within your range of control and correction. By studying the nuances of the qualities of the *sephirot* and observing how well you are developing these qualities within yourself, you become a more capable co-creator of the world. Our mystics say that the *Omer* season *sephirot* studies, along with the many other methods they have developed for cultivating the balance and flow of awareness from one *sephirah* to another within you, have an effect on the Whole Enterprise of Being.

There are many practices for steadily cultivating your Tree of Life consciousness throughout the year. For example,

- Each *sephirah* has a color associated with it. You may have noticed a prayer shawl, a tallit, on the market that has rainbow stripes as its design. The prototype for this tallit was developed by Reb Zalman for use during meditation in preparation for prayer.
- One of the most ancient of our meditation practices is the wearing of *tefillin*, leather straps with little boxes containing the Shema and other excerpts from Torah within them. These are worn

so that these prayers are set near your head and your heart. Each of the seven windings of the *tefillin* on your arm can be done as a meditation on one of the *sephirot*.

- As your practice advances, studying the correlations the ancients developed between the lives of the ancestors and the qualities of the *sephirot* is also helpful. This study can also be incorporated into the *ushpizin* process that we studied in the section on *Sukkot* (page 54–55).
- When you arrive at the time of counting the *Omer*, your individual attention to the *sephirot* during the year will be magnified by pairing them for in-depth study during the *Omer* process.

RECIPE # 27
The *Omer*
Process

Each day of the *Omer*—the forty-nine days from Passover to Shavuot—has a *sephirah* assigned to it, and each week also has one, so that every day has a pair, to be considered one in relation to the other.

- We begin with the *Omer* blessing: *Baruḥ atah adonai eloheynu meleḥ ha olam, asher kidshanu b'mitzvotav, v'tzivanu al sefirat ha-omer,* "regarding the counting of the Omer."
- Look at the *Omer* calendar that follows and take note of which two qualities intersect on day twenty-four of the *Omer*.

- Now look up the nuances of those qualities in the listing above.
- Did you find the answer to be *tiferet* in association with *netzah?* So the study opportunity on Day 24 is the discussion and contemplation of how "compassion functions within endurance" in your life.
- Discussing each day's combination with friends, family, and an *Omer* study partner will greatly deepen the value of this practice for you, as will keeping an *Omer* journal.
- Here's an example of my journal reflection for Day 31 of the *Omer* this past year:
  "Hmm. When I am trying to stay with something, finish writing a section, complete a painting, focus on a one-on-one conversation, how do I react to others around me who want attention? Sometimes feisty or gruff or oblivious. Can I become aware of others during such times and find a sweet way to let them know I will be able to be present in a little while, more so than right now? I am aware that I must set boundaries during my writing times, and I am aware that this requires sacrifice on the part of my dear ones. Today is dedicated to noticing and starting to implement the potential in this pairing of compassion with endurance. May I be blessed to continue to evolve."

THE *OMER* CALENDER OF THE JEWISH MYSTICS
Counting starts on the second night of Passover

Hesed	*Gevurah*	*Tiferet*	*Netzah*	*Hod*	*Yesod*	*Malhut*
1 *Hesed*	2 *Hesed*	3 *Hesed*	4 *Hesed*	5 *Hesed*	6 *Hesed*	7 *Hesed*
8 *Gevurah*	9 *Gevurah*	10 *Gevurah*	11 *Gevurah*	12 *Gevurah*	13 *Gevurah*	14 *Gevurah*
15 *Tiferet*	16 *Tiferet*	17 *Tiferet*	18 *Tiferet*	19 *Tiferet*	20 *Tiferet*	21 *Tiferet*
22 *Netzah*	23 *Netzah*	24 *Netzah*	25 *Netzah*	26 *Netzah*	27 *Netzah*	28 *Netzah*
29 *Hod*	30 *Hod*	31 *Hod*	32 *Hod*	33 *Hod*	34 *Hod*	35 *Hod*
36 *Yesod*	37 *Yesod*	38 *Yesod*	39 *Yesod*	40 *Yesod*	41 *Yesod*	42 *Yesod*
43 *Malhut*	44 *Malhut*	45 *Malhut*	46 *Malhut*	47 *Malhut*	48 *Malhut*	49 *Malhut*

THE *SEPHIROT* AND ASSOCIATED PATTERNS							
Hesed	Gevurah	Tiferet	Netza_h_	Hod	Yesod	Mal_h_ut	
Ultra-violet	Blue	Green	Yellow	Orange	Red	Brown	Colors
Abraham Miriam	Isaac Leah	Jacob Hannah	Moses Rebecca	Aaron Sarah	Joseph Tamar	David Rachel	Ancestors

Note: Variations may be found in these matters. You might wish to explore other systems; see what works for you.

What if you accidentally skip *Omer* practice for a day? Forgive yourself; it's not a sin, it's a practice. Do some catch-up and stay in the sequence as scheduled. Others you meet may be following this same practice, and you might want to exchange thoughts about the implications of the pair for the day. One year, at a meeting of my women's monthly Rosh Ḥodesh, "new moon," gathering, it was *Omer* time. The day's sephirotic combination was the *Gevurah* of *Hod*, which we discussed as "strengthening containment." Each person imagined what kind of container she might be and how to strengthen that quality in herself. Very helpful!

As you study the pairs and refine your awareness of your own polarities, you will become a renewed person, better able to serve as a conduit for life. Each day is a small step on the road to higher consciousness, your own way of arriving at Sinai.

OBSTACLES ON THE JOURNEY

According to talmudic and midrashic sources, at the time of the Roman Empire twenty-four thousand disciples of the sage Rabbi Akiva died from a plague during the period between Passover and Shavuot. The sages attributed this plague to negative internal politics among Akiva's students, saying: "They did not sufficiently honor one another." To drive home the importance of refraining from toxic communal politics, this negative event is remembered through the sobering *Omer* practice of holding no weddings or other celebrations, and making no festive preparations for Shavuot, such as getting haircuts and shaving, until Day 33 of the *Omer*.

LAG B'OMER

The thirty-third day of the *Omer* is a festival known as Lag b'Omer, named by the phonetic sound of the number thirty-three in Hebrew. On this day it is customary to light bonfires and engage in ecstatic dancing and mystical studies in honor of the *yahrzeit*, anniversary, of the death of the luminary of Jewish mysticism, Rabbi Shimon bar Yoḥai. He is also known by the acronym Rashbi. On the day of his death Rabbi Shimon was reported to have become suffused by a great, radiant light that also filled his home as he revealed the final secrets of his mystical practices.

Rashbi is traditionally considered to be the primary author of the Jewish mystical text known as the Zohar, which means "radiance." In his honor, Lag b'Omer marks an end to the *Omer* restrictions on celebrations described earlier. Many of Rabbi Shimon's teachings shed great light on a core tenet of Judaism: our capacity to evolve as people, which is reflected

in a number of special customs for children and families prevalent on this day, including:

- Bonfire sculptures. In Israel and increasingly in
  other parts of the world, children collect wood for
  bonfires in anticipation of the festival and pile the
  wood into interesting sculptures.
- Bonfire parties of many types. Family barbecues or
  ecstatic fireside study gatherings blaze with intensity across the land of Israel and around the world,
  with the largest on Mt. Meron in Sefat, at the
  gravesites of Rabbi Shimon bar Yohai and his son,
  Rabbi Eleazar.
- Pretend hunting bows and arrows for children. Our
  folklore tells that Rabbi Akiva and his students,
  when confronted by a Roman law against Torah
  study at penalty of death, would dress up for
  hunting and head into the forest to study. Today,
  some people give children tiny bow-and-arrow sets
  with suction cups for arrow points and recount this
  tale of the courage it sometimes takes to study
  Torah. Since some children remove the suction
  cups, extensive supervision is necessary for this
  activity, or else a visit to a professional archery
  range can be great fun when coupled with the story.
- Upsherin. On Lag b'Omer thousands of parents
  bring their three-year-olds to Mt. Meron or to
  the graves of other mystical sages or hold a home-
  based ritual for their first haircut. This practice
  has fascinating roots and is of both practical and
  spiritual importance.

What a curious time to select for first haircuts for pre-schoolers! The reason is quite inspiring and requires us to look into a story found in the Talmud Tractate Shabbat 33b, which reveals how even the great Rabbi Shimon bar Yoḥai once had to be given a massive time-out for wrongly using the power of his spirit.

Our story takes place at the time when the Romans had made the study of Torah illegal. Rabbi Shimon spoke out publicly against this injustice and was sentenced to death. By various clever means he was able to get to a cave in northern Israel, where he hid with his son for twelve years. They occupied themselves all that time with Torah study. In this cave there appeared a carob tree that served as a food, a stream for water, and a sand-and-mud pit for warmth.

When the prevailing Caesar died, the decree against Rabbi Shimon was lifted and he and his son soon left the cave. They came upon Jewish farmers working in a field. Rabbi Shimon was so unaccustomed to the real world and the idea of Jews who were not occupied in Torah study so distressed him that he vaporized the Jewish farms and farmers with his gaze. A voice from heaven immediately called out, "My world is not to be destroyed. Return to your cave!"

Therein father and son stayed for another year until the voice returned, allowing them to emerge. They did so on a Friday afternoon, when people were, of course, engaged in mundane as well as Shabbat preparation activities. When a man hurried past bearing two bunches of myrtle blossoms Rabbi Shimon and his son inquired as to where he was going with the flowers.

"For the honor of Shabbat," he replied.

"But why two?" they asked.

"One for *shamor* (observing the laws of Shabbat) and one for *zahor* (remembering the beautiful experience of the gift of Shabbat)," the man responded.

Rabbi Shimon replied, "Now I can see the power of a Jew and mitzvot."

Notice that Rabbi Shimon met a man carrying myrtle leaves—surely this is a symbol meant to catch our attention. Our sages note the myrtle leaf is shaped like an eye; indeed we are watching Rabbi Shimon to see if he has learned, or will another time-out be given? Notice how differently Rabbi Shimon handled this second encounter. He has learned to *shamor*, observe, to be curious, to drop the judgment. He can now *zahor*, remember the lesson taught to him, and not replicate his rage.

Shamor and *zahor*, achieved by "observing" the deep structure of tradition through "remembering" to thoughtfully apply the spirit of the Torah's intent. Rabbi Shimon had studied the structure but lost contact with the meaning. Balance is required by G*d of this sage and also is an important component of our own spiritual health. This story of Rabbi Shimon can be read as a parable about maturation and about parenting, including a cameo episode of Cosmic Parenting. In this story the voice of G*d comes to teach that healthy boundaries are as required of our sages, as of ourselves.

Many metaphors can be found in this story that are really portals to a higher parenting consciousness. For example, a person is often likened to a tree in the Torah: "A person is like the tree of a field" (Deuteronomy 20:19). Hence, the carob tree in our parable. Jewish law requires that baby trees be allowed to develop for three years before the fruit is harvested from their limbs. This concept is called *orlah* (Leviticus

19:23). Just as a young tree needs developmental freedom, we try to create safe space for babies to playfully develop with few limits other than those needed for safety. And let's not forget that time of the "terrible twos," preceding the breath of relief usually brought by the change in cognitive and behavioral ability of a child of age three.

The *upsherin* haircutting ritual helps us acknowledge that children are like young trees at three, better able to tolerate guidance as they come into the ability to learn, retain, and replicate behaviors with consciousness. It can be hard to let go of the image of one's child as "baby," and to embrace the idea of a child able to take direction who is soon to attend pre-school.

Also in our parable, a stream comes up beside the carob tree. Torah is often compared to water: "May my teaching drop like the rain" (Deuteronomy 32:2) and a person is "like a tree planted near water" (Jeremiah 17:8). This reflection of the Cosmic Parent is also the prayer of teachers and parents, that the guidance and Torah we offer our youth will have the life-giving effect of water.

Another reference in Torah to *orlah* is about the form of pruning known as circumcision, a physical reminder of the importance in Judaism to maintain healthy sexual boundaries and activity, and to fulfill our ethical covenant forged at Sinai through dedication to learning for living through Torah study. Perhaps this particular *orlah* reference reveals one reason why, until very recently, *upsherin* was exclusively a ritual for male children.

And yet, the sand, mud, and darkness in our parable cut Rabbi Shimon and his son off from the grounding and wisdom to be gained through farming and other vital societal activities of daily living. Torah study in the dark, removed from the reality of society proves to be dangerous. Rabbi Shimon and his son emerge somewhat like babies from a womb, eyes not yet reopened to the needs of others. This story is often used in traditional communities to state the case for the importance of balancing Torah study with remunerative and charitable work in the world.

Continued study of this tale can yield many more powerful parenting metaphors and principles. Perhaps study of this text can prove a useful way for parents and educators to prepare for such transitions themselves.

Day thirty-three of the *Omer* is a traditional time to hold a haircutting party ritual to commemorate a Jewish child's first haircut, which is generally not done until about three years of age. The *upsherin* ritual itself is simple, and as in every mitzvah, it is yours to elaborate as desired, keeping in mind age-appropriate length and activities.

RECIPE # 28
Upsherin: A Coming-of-Age Ritual for Toddlers and Their Families

- Gather friends and family for a bonfire or barbecue. Keep in mind the dictum that it is wise to invite no more young people to a party than the child's current age. It is also helpful for the child to have seen others enjoying getting haircuts and to have practiced on a doll in advance.
- Age three is when a child traditionally can begin to wear a *tallit-katan* (a lightweight undergarment with *tzitzit,* fringes that are reminders to live a

mitzvah-centered life) and a *kippah*. These items
are usually presented privately to the child so that
they can be donned without stress and with excite-
ment at wearing what big kids wear.

- It is traditional to give a first lesson in Hebrew letters on this day. You might begin by having those
attending the ritual sing the Hebrew alphabet, or
the traditional verse from Deuteronomy 33:4 for
upsherin: "The Torah was commanded to us through
Moses, an inheritance for all the Jewish people."
This verse in Hebrew begins: *Torah Tziva Lanu
Moshe* and is an acronym for *tzelem*, "image." This
special day is meant to leave a positive image with
the child of a first connection with Torah study in a
sweet and fun way. See www.ReclaimingJudaism.org
for helpful sources of Jewish music resources on
the web.

- A brief speech describing changes and how you feel
about them might be given here. This is a time when
the child is more mobile, less tolerant of hugging and
holding; a time for parents to firmly set and maintain
boundaries. A big emotional and behavioral state
change is also being marked for the parent(s).

- The first snip is taken in the area of the bangs, at
the place where the head *tefillin* box is meant to sit,
on what is called the Third Eye in eastern religions, and is a place of wisdom and vision in
Jewish tradition.

- In some communities a sage, if one is present,
might be asked to speak briefly and cut the first
lock of hair.

- Traditional and some liberal-creative families may follow the practice of leaving *payis*, side locks, as the longest remaining hair. These are reminders to live a mitzvah-centered life, as in the story of Ruth, where the poor glean from what is intentionally left on the side of the fields for them. Others only do a token snipping at the *upsherin* and take the child to a formal hair salon later in the day for a professional cut. This is a matter of personal inclination.
- If it feels right for the personality and mood of a given child, those present can each take a turn snipping off a lock of hair. Or, have a professional present to complete the haircut so that the tresses can be properly harvested and donated to an organization that makes wigs for children with cancer, such as Locks of Love.
- After the haircut the youngster might give a solo rendition of *Torah Tziva Lanu* or another Hebrew song.
- Now, a sweet—sometimes honey on the edge of a slip of paper with a verse of Torah on it—is brought to the child to be licked off, as a memory of the sweetness of growing old enough to start preschool and begin learning. Others give a laminated Hebrew letter card from an alphabet deck with something sweet on it, or perhaps with a lollipop on top.
- Guests then bless the child with spontaneous hopes for a future close to Torah and the sweetness of Jewish practice and sing some more.

Our young tree has been pruned in a beautiful rite of passage. Now it's time for some real fruit and food—everybody eat!

REALLY, AN ALL-NIGHTER?

The *Omer* period leads right up to the eve of Shavuot. To stay up all night studying Judaism in community is an important practice on that night. This is called engaging in a *Tikkun Leyl Shavuot. Tikkun* means, "repair," for the *leyl,* "night of" Shavuot. The principle is to be as open as possible to hearing Torah in new ways that might prove healing for the world. It is most interesting to see what various communities have to offer in the way of subject matter. One year my husband and I were in New York City on *erev* Shavuot we went to B'nai Jeshurun to study mystical and meditation texts from Ḥasidic, Kabbalistic, and feminist sources. Other synagogues, however, offered options such as: "Learn whether it is permissible to send an express mail letter right before Shabbat begins"; "Should you fast on Friday to make Shabbat more special?" Or, at another facility: "Does archeological evidence support the reality of the Exodus? Consider intertextual evidence that the Torah has many authors." And at yet another: "*Tikkun* means repair: All night tonight we will consider what major efforts can be made to repair community relations between ethnic groups in our neighborhood."

Although the options are many, their goal is always the same, to arrive at Shavuot as a community of souls open to hearing the Torah as new and fresh. To discuss the torah of each other's lives and thoughts all night in relation to core texts and greet the dawn as a community can be a transformational process both for individuals and for an evolving Jewish community.

Select a warm and comfortable place in the synagogue or at someone's home.

- Have refreshments available—pot luck is good—to see you through the night.
- Have extra pillows available and encourage people to bring sleeping bags. People will drift off to sleep for periods of time. That's allowed. This is not a cult; it's an opportunity.
- A few weeks in advance, invite members of the community to take twenty-minute slots, bringing texts on whatever theme your community has selected this year, or simply talking about whatever subject they choose, as long as it is connected to Torah.
- Begin with the blessing for Torah study, which, after the traditional opening, finishes with *la-asok b'divrei Torah*, "to immerse yourself in words of Torah."
- Encourage song, dance, drama, art, storytelling, *hevruta*, "study with a partner." Make it a multimodality time; stimulate all the senses.
- Consider holding a sunrise service. When you step up for an *aliyah*, many new meanings of Torah may dawn.

RECIPE # 29
A Spiritual
All-Nighter:
*Tikkun Leyl
Shavuot*

ENTERING SHAVUOT

On Shavuot we move from being people on the run to a people with a plan. No longer are we focused on complaining about our past partners in civilization and their oppressive ways. We're refocused on changing ourselves. Humbled by the challenges of learning how to live in the wilderness phase of a new life, we are open to guidance.

Major changes require questioning all dearly held assumptions. What will be the ethics of your new life? What culture? Boundaries? Norms? What order do you want to consciously create in your new life? From where will help and guidance come?

The long days of learning the hard way progress until we realize that more than mere survival is possible. It might be an upward climb, but there's more, much more, that is possible. And we are going to be a different kind of society, if only we can focus our ideas and really hear what's possible. On Shavuot we know we're standing at the base of the mountain, open to guidance. When it comes, we know it for the revelation it is, a template for sane living expressed in the form of Torah.

For those who study Torah intensively as a daily part of the fabric of living, Shavuot is a passionate moment of connection to its birth. For those who don't study Torah regularly, Shavuot can become a time to deepen awareness of the impact and meaning it has and can have in your life. Part of what Torah is, is how people use it. To be able to speak as an empowered person who has one's own personal relationship to the Bible can be very important in this world of ours.

Every year on Shavuot, as part of the commitment ritual of our peoplehood, Moses again brings down the tablets, carrying the Architect's newest blueprint for collective living. We become again a people, the Jewish people, agreeing to become the builders of a civilization based on a plan called Torah, and to dwell within it. Like all blueprints, this one also is a V.O.S., "verify on site," situation. Living conditions must be assessed and, without destroying the integrity of the design, we must take responsibility for the on-site evolution of the details so that the plan continues to serve every generation.

Shavuot is the recognition of the value of
ethical freedom over anarchy.

Shavuot is a radical realization in the wilderness;
Civilization *is* a spiritual practice.
Shavuot is the celebration
of a diverse people joining together in the wilderness,
choosing to enter a unifying covenant
under the identity of *children of Israel*,
today called the *Jewish people*.

Agreeing to live in a conscious partnership with
no single idol, king, being, or false G*d,
but rather to partner reality with the Mystery
that resists labels, saying in Exodus at the burning bush:
Ehyeh asher Ehyeh, "I will be what I will be"

How can we help with this great becoming?
Through being attuned to
principles and memories,
received as instructions for living,
called *Torah*.

WHY THE SCROLL OF RUTH?

Shavuot is about more than your personal development; it is about the formation of the Jewish people from a mixed multitude of diverse humans who became bound together by the common experience of slavery followed by a collective wilderness adventure. They realize they have become a family, the children of Israel. Because of this, Shavuot has added significance for those who have converted or who are converting to Judaism, a significance that is intensified by the traditional reading of the Book of Ruth. In the story, Naomi and her husband, Elimele_h_, emigrate with their two sons from the Israelite land of Judah to Moab. Naomi's husband dies, and her two sons die as well, leaving Naomi and her two Moabite daughters-in-law, Orpah and Ruth.

Naomi, who has decided to return to her own people in Judah, encourages her native daughters-in-law to remain in their land of origin under the protection of their families. The bond among the women, transcending any national differences, is, however, intensely close. Both Orpah and Ruth want to go with her, even though, without family support, they will live as women at risk and as paupers. To survive they will need to glean from the sides of the fields, a tenet of charitable sharing turned into a principle of Jewish law in the Talmud.

Ultimately, Orpah agrees to remain in Moab, to "return to her own people and her G*d," but Ruth will not, and she utters the now-famous words from Ruth 1:16–17: "Wherever you go, I will go. Wherever you lodge, I will lodge. Your people shall be my people. Your G*d my G*d. Where you die, I will die. There I will be buried."

I have often seen those who have converted to Judaism crying during the reading of the Book of Ruth. Notice that it is not called the Book of Naomi or even of Boaz, whom Ruth meets on the threshing floor and who becomes her Israelite husband. It is not easy to become a Jew; we don't have instant conversions. There is a process of admission involving extensive study and serious ritual. Not everyone is meant to be Jewish in this life. If your soul needs it, however, it is my experience that nothing will stop you from finding your way in. Currently more than 200,000 North Americans raised on other paths have become Jews by choice.

> The Book of Ruth is named in honor of
> a woman who joined our people.
> From her lineage will descend King David.
> To wholeheartedly
> join your destiny to the Jewish people
> is to both receive and contribute to
> sustaining a living Torah
> by adding your vision, views,
> voice, values, and lineage
> to the people and practices
> your soul chooses to call home.

9

Yom HaShoah, Yom HaAtzmaut, and Tisha b'Av
Healing from the Hard Knocks of History

The stunning frequency of Jews being massacred, deported, and exiled is given serious space, though not a front seat, in our holy day cycle. Great courage is required to carry the important principles contained within Judaism forward into the human future. Our people's spirit contains much joy and determination and also sadness, fear, and lingering mourning from many horrific events.

> Our people have remarkable coping mechanisms,
> including the ability to boundary grief
> in favor of savoring life.
> We do this by creating a container in time,
> the rare addition of a new holy day,
> dedicated to the memorial and integration
> of extreme loss and profound trauma.

Two major sequences on the Jewish calendar are appointed to the essential tasks of collective mourning, memorial, reflection, and renewal. One began in the first century to commemorate the Babylonian exile of our people from our homeland; the other in the twentieth century, due to the attempted genocide of our exiled people by the Nazis and their collaborators in what is termed in Hebrew *Shoah*, "utter devastation," the Holocaust.

SEQUENCE ONE: COPING WITH THE DESTRUCTION OF THE TEMPLE AND EXILE

Scholars estimate that one fifth of all Jews died in our struggle for independence from Rome, by siege, slaughter, starvation, crucifixion, being sold as gladiators or slaves, in direct battle, or by fire in the burning city. Over time, this date has accrued memories of hundreds of thousands of Jews murdered: during the three centuries of the Crusades, including the expulsion of the Jews from England in 1290; over three hundred fifty years of the Spanish Inquisition; in the 1648 Chmielnicki massacres in the Ukraine of some one hundred thousand Jews; and many other murderous rampages called *pogroms* that decimated Jewish communities in Eastern Europe.

Practices in this sequence include:

- A daylight fast is held on the seventeenth of the lunar month of Tammuz, marking the breaching of the walls of Jerusalem by the Roman conquerors.
- A full fast day on the ninth of Av, the date of the destruction of the Temple in Jerusalem by the Babylonian Empire in 586 B.C.E., and by the Romans in 70 C.E.

- *Eihah*, the Book of Lamentations, became a holy repository for the anguished memories from the destruction of the Temple and exile and has been canonized as the sacred text to be chanted on Tisha b'Av.
- Traditionally, from the first until the fifteenth of the lunar month of Av (which usually falls in July or August) Jews hold no weddings, nor do we attend movies, musical festivities, or plays. Beards remain unshaven and hair uncut, except to honor Shabbat. Shabbat is a "now" experience that transcends all, lest we lose touch with the Big Picture of the great evolving and healing ever-present in life.
- On Tisha b'Av, the ninth of Av, there is full fasting—no water, beverages, or food, unless a health condition requires them. In Judaism, your health comes first! In some parts of the world, people wear sackcloth and ashes and sit on the floor on low benches, as in mourning. On this day Torah is not studied for pleasure, only portions pertinent to Tisha b'Av themes are to be read, perhaps to simulate a world turned upside down. In some communities *tallit* and *tefillin* are worn in the afternoon and not in the morning.
- The days between the seventeenth of Tammuz and Tisha b'Av are referred to as *beyn ha-metzarim*, "between the narrow straits," a place of painful constriction. As is said in Yiddish, it is *shver zolzein a Yid*, "hard to be a Jew."
- Historical records reveal that after conquering Jerusalem and the Temple and only partially exiling

the Jewish people, the Babylonian armies return. They return because of Jewish infighting; the Jewish governor, whom the Babylonians had left in place, is assassinated by another Jew. This results in an extremely brutal and much more extensive exile of Jews from the land. In memory of this tragedy another partial fast called *Tsom Gedaliah*, named after the murdered governor, is observed several weeks after Tisha b'Av. Even so, in every generation, some Jews have managed to remain in Israel. The poorest of the Jewish farmers are recorded in the Bible as having been left in residence to till the land for the Babylonian conquerors after the destruction of the Temple.

To remember where it hurts,
how it got that way,
to tell the journey,
to honor the pain,
not become the story.

To keen, wail, let out the anger and grief,
to express the desire to have things go back
to the way they once were; *hahdeysh yahmenu k'kedem*
to *shrei gevalt*—"to cry out: ENOUGH!"

Tisha b'Av is a time for mourning our exiles—from Jerusalem, from self, from safe and supportive co-existence with other nations, from relationship with G*d. It is a time for considering the consequences of having been driven out of our homes so often in history, families torn apart. The sadness of this day is huge. It is the sadness of knowing that humans can be inhumane, that your life can be imperiled irrationally and that murderous waves of anti-Semitism can sweep into your life en masse. Intrinsic to Judaism will always be an element of mourning, because we know these lessons too well.

A word also found in the story of Noah in Genesis is found in the Book of Lamentations: *hamas*—all-encompassing violence, total devastation. In Lamentations it takes the emphatic (infinitive absolute) verb form, and the lament describes this *hamas* as coming from the *meleh*, a masculine noun used to refer to the impersonal Cosmos-creating aspect of what Jewish mystics mean when speaking of G*d. At the same time, the interpersonal, caring, feminine noun *Shehinah* is the aspect of G*d that suffers with us and is spoken of as walking out into exile as a mourner with Her people.

A spiritual question implicit in Tisha b'Av becomes: In what way is the *Shehinah* in exile now, in our lives, communities, countries, actions? How do we re-create the intent of the word Jerusalem, *Yeru/shalem*? Its name is a hope and prayer for a *Y'ru*, "city of," *Shalem*, "completeness, wholeness, fulfillment, peace."

The Hebrew title of the Book of Lamentations is *Eihah*, which means "How." It derives from the first line of the text, "How lonely are we." To lament means to mourn or wail. Pick up a copy of Lamentations, look at the words with a friend, go line by line to see how the verses apply to you in your life. What is your lament?

RECIPE # 30
Writing
Lamentations:
When Life
Gives You
Grief

Lamentations is a sacred text.
Your laments are also holy.
Lamenting is part of the initial process
of healing from a wounding.
Sometimes you can become stuck in that place,
playing the same tape over and over.

A lament must be
heard, honored, and looked into
to see what you need.

When a lament moves on to become
part of your sacred history,
no longer in the foreground of your daily life,
then healing has begun.

Laments are often mishandled. A nursing home resident laments, "I had a beautiful home; my children sold it. Now I live in a small room; the meals here do not taste right." Too often the response is, "You are so lucky to be here. This is an excellent facility. You couldn't live on your own any more." To respect a lament, however, is to respond, "How sad you sound to have given up your home and so much of your independence. I can imagine that you miss the familiar taste of foods you preferred, and there are many other things you probably miss, too." If heard and respected, the pattern of the lament does not have to be repeated, and curiosity about being in a new place with different advantages will have room to emerge.

This, too, is the function of Lamentations on Tisha b'Av; for the pain of the ancestors to be heard and honored, the hard lessons reviewed and grasped, so we can move on with renewed vigor and determination for living.

I first encountered this technique for experiencing the meaning of a text in a *midrash* class taught by the choreographer Liz Lerman. This works best if done with a study group or class.

RECIPE # 31
Empathy through Enactment

- In one page, write out your worst nightmare or invent a worst-nightmare scenario.
- Keeping them anonymous, unsigned, have everyone place these paragraphs on the floor around the room.
- Wander among them, reading and capturing key phrases that can be expressed in a movement of your arms, head, and body. For example, when I first did this, I saw that someone had written about a car wreck, rolling over and over in a vehicle that was out of control. I began to roll on the floor, feeling terror. Another described being trapped in the freezing cold on a camping trip; I let those words wrack my body with shivers. Someone else wrote of being a Jew asking everyone in her village to help her during the war and their acting as if they could not see her. So I wandered the room begging invisible villagers for help. The woman beside me enacted a miscarriage caused by an assault. An Israeli woman's page was about being in a marketplace when a car bomb exploded and

shrapnel tore through her leg. My father's leg was crushed when he served as an Allied soldier in World War II; I stared down, gaping at my own uninjured extremity.

- In small groups of three to four people, share these movements—rolling out of control, shaking, begging, and many more.
- Now choreograph the movements into a sequence.
- Now enact the sequence while someone reads or chants from the Book of Lamentations.

Become the mourners streaming out of Jerusalem, your daughters ravaged, your guts spilling out, and your faith a torment. Become Tisha b'Av.

Some thought to put an end to this mourning sequence when the State of Israel was reborn.
We didn't. We cannot forget Jerusalem fell twice before.
From memory comes determination and strength.

YOM HASHOAH, YOM HAZIKARON, YOM HAATZMAUT

A second sequence of mourning and renewal was required when the needs of the remnant of displaced, devastated, and still homeless Jewish people bled through the heart the awareness of humanity, so that by the conclusion of World War II:

- The United Nations formally affirmed the re-establishment of a Jewish homeland as the State of Israel to commence on May 15, 1948, and Yom

HaAtzmaut, Israel Independence Day, is celebrated around the twenty-first day of the Omer. (Can vary slightly based on lunar month cycles and practice of avoiding holding this on Shabbat.)

- Our experience of hope and re-emergence from oppression was promptly challenged by the renewed nation being attacked by the surrounding nations. The world watched as the fragment of our people who survived World War II mounted a defense. One percent of Israelis died in the thirteen-month war for independence that ensued. Israel miraculously survived to once again take on the joys and challenges of nationhood.

- Yom HaZikaron, the fifth of Iyar, is set aside to memorialize Israel's ever-mounting war dead and missing-in-action, and is held the day before Israel Independence Day. In Israel's military cemeteries many tombstones are sculptures of beds, and on Yom HaZikaron families throughout the country can be found weeping upon them. A siren sounds on this day and for two minutes everyone stops what they are doing to stand in a silent tribute and within that, one mother told me, she silently screams, "Why?"

- Holocaust Memorial Day, known as Yom HaShoah (*Shoah* means "utter devastation") is designated by Israel's parliament for Omer, day twelve, proximal to the anniversary of the Warsaw Ghetto Uprising and yet not fall during Passover. It took time to recognize that the enormity of this tragedy required more space than simple incorporation into Tisha b'Av. So within the Omer sequence is this additional experience of Yom HaShoah, Yom HaZikaron, and Yom HaAtzmaut.

- On Yom HaShoah respectful pluralism comes naturally, as many join the Jewish people in mourning and remembering the over 11 million people whom the Nazis and their collaborators murdered during the Holocaust. This number includes six million Jews and five million additional target group members: homosexuals, gypsies, mental patients, the developmentally disabled, deformed and handicapped persons, political prisoners, Jehovah's Witnesses, black Germans, Poles, and Russian prisoners of war.

RETELLING THE UNIMAGINABLE

Yom HaShoah observations have at their core a retelling and remembering. As one who personally worked with survivors, I undertake the mitzvah of doing so now. A woman came into my office at the Jewish Federation in the 1980s, carrying a yellowed square of a German newspaper.

"You are head of things here?" she inquired.

"Yes."

"So you must guard this for the future."

"What does it say?" I asked. "I don't yet read German."

She shook her head and gently whispered, "I entrust it to you." She left quickly.

I went across the hall to the insurance office run by another German-Jewish survivor. He translated it for me. It was taken from a small-town paper listing the deaths of a number of children in a town named Auschwitz.

I went to her house and she let me in. I sat at her table and she told me the clipping was from the day after her children were separated from her in line at the concentration camp; this for her was their obituary. She told me she had hidden with them for twenty months in numerous non-Jewish "safe" houses in Germany until a man informed on her and the children to save his own life. Her husband had died early in the war; I don't recall how.

In America, she met and married another survivor and was surprised with a late-life pregnancy and birth of a healthy daughter. The next day I told my board of the incident. An adult child of a survivor responded to my request to tape the woman's story in depth by, within forty-eight hours, raising money from other children of survivors to fully equip a small independent archive project. From those difficult days of excruciating listening and asking, one story in particular still holds my soul in a vise, the only one where the teller required that we stop the camera.

"You must retell this yourself," he instructed me. I ask forgiveness of his soul for any way my memory may differ from his original telling.

A pre-teen during the war, in the Riga Ghetto; now, an elder. He narrated to me the narrowing of the ghetto, the crowding of people closer and closer, many families crammed into single apartments and a few streets and of his watching columns of the Jews of Riga being marched to the Black Forest to be shot and buried.

His father was a pharmacist and secreted stockpiles of medicines around the ghetto, thus becoming precious to the Nazis as a source of antibiotics and antiseptics. His father was shot dead on the street one night while bringing medicine to another Jewish family. Thus he, the son, became the source of medicine. He used the power of his knowledge of the many secret stashes and shared with the Nazis in small increments. The Nazis never knew whether he had more hidden somewhere else, so they let him live as they drained the ghetto of life.

After many hours, in the monotone of traumatic memory, he spoke to me of watching his mother dragged out and forced into the columns being marched to the forest. Then he made me abruptly stop the camera, saying this was the end of his interview.

His wife, who elected to be in the room during tapings, came over to comfort him. He seemed to me to be in a condition unlike the other survivors, who appeared unburdened by the telling. His face and body were tight and controlled. He sobbed out, "There's more. Keep the camera off. If you tell this it must be from you alone, not the tape; you who see me, you alone will retell the end."

We sat down, he looked like death. What I recall him saying was that a group of young women with infants were in hiding in a cellar; young and small, he could bring them medicines, bits of food and water. When the ghetto was down to a very few streets the mothers surrounded him and asked for a drug that would allow them to poison the babies so they could die in peace in their mothers' arms, not shot in the forest, perhaps to lie bleeding to death in pain. He was only a boy, he didn't know what to do. For days he tried to convince them differently.

Each day in the ghetto more and more residents were marched out in the columns; he used the expression "the columns" so that it held the most dread of any term I'd ever heard.

Finally, he gave them a vial of the drug he hoped would lead to a quick and merciful death for the infants. The mothers surrendered themselves to the Nazis with their dead babies in their arms.

Let this telling be over, I silently prayed. But there was more.

Days passed. He was made to pack furniture onto trucks and was able to leave the ghetto with the furnishings, ultimately to jump the truck, escape, and eventually be captured, placed in a concentration camp, and survive. He turned to me saying in the greatest anguish I hope ever to see in a human, "You see, I who survived, I am a murderer . . . who knows how many of them might have survived if not for me?"

Every year on Yom HaShoah I undertake and need the ritual of saying Kaddish for all of them, the three- and four-year-olds who were informed on, the father and mother of the burdened young boy, the young women and their infants, and most recently for the boy himself who had lived to have a wonderful family, solid career, and a long life. In his time of turmoil, would we have acted differently? How does one know when or whether to end suffering? *Zichronam l'vrakhah*, may their memories be for a blessing.

Extreme soul anguish accompanies the devastation of whole cities in war, and a toxic loss of trust suffuses survivors of mass death wrought through violence bred of irrational hatred. Only since the 9/11 terrorist attacks, and discovering our own need for a day and rituals of memorial, have some of us born on American soil after World War II come to grasp a very small sense of what it is to live in such times.

Many forms of Holocaust memorial have begun to emerge— museums, paintings, books, archives, research institutes, and

more. This too is part of healing, the encasing of memory.
Major rituals for Yom HaShoah include:

- Israel passed a law in 1961 that closed all public
  entertainment on Yom HaShoah. A siren sounds
  at ten in the morning, everyone stops what they
  are doing, those in cars pull over, get out, and
  stand in remembrance. Throughout the world
  some people also choose to abstain from entertainment and to follow the basic rituals of a fast
  day—abstaining from wearing leather, shaving,
  wearing make-up, or adorning oneself—but not
  fasting, for to emulate the suffering of those in the
  camps feels inappropriate.
- "Unto every person there is a name" is an initiative
  of the Holocaust Museum in Israel, Yad Vashem,
  which provides lists of the names of Jewish victims
  for memorial rituals. In many communities six candles are lit to represent the six million who died
  and lengthy (sometimes twenty-four-hour) name-
  readings of victims are conducted. For example, at
  the site of the former Velodrome d'Hiver, where
  Parisian Jews were concentrated for deportation,
  there is an annual reading of names of the French
  Jewish deportees.
- Curricula on tolerance and how to stand up to
  injustice are often dedicated and donated to
  schools on this date. It is essential to teach our
  children, without frightening them, about what
  occurred. Is this happening in your community?

- The annual "March of the Living" brings together thousands of youth from around the world during April of each year to participate in a ceremonial march from the concentration camp Auschwitz I to Birkenau.

- Many light one yellow memorial candle at home on Yom HaShoah. A project of the Federation of Jewish Men's Clubs (www.FJMC.org), this action creates an experience of an altar of consciousness in your home, to which prayer, discussion, and memories can be added. Congregation Beth David in Saratoga, California, has expanded upon this by wrapping around the yellow candles a map of the many sites of Jewish resistance to deportation and slaughter, and sending this home with Hebrew school students to families along with recommended readings and rituals.

- Of all the diverse ways of responding and remembering, it is the need to gather in community for comfort, mourning, and reflection that is becoming firmly established in the calendar of Jewish sacred time. Yom HaShoah memorial services rarely have the usual infrastructure of a traditional Jewish prayer service—no Shema, no *amidah*, no *aleynu*. These commemorations are not about praising G*d, nor could they be, when anger is all that many have left of any relationship with G*d.

- As the survivors among us age and their souls depart, a need has emerged for a sacred text to recount the tragedy, much as Lamentations is chanted on Tisha b'Av. A poignant work called

Megillat HaShoah: The Shoah Scroll has emerged via the Conservative Movement (www.USCJ.org) that seems to fulfill with power and dignity this huge and awesome task.

The survivors who set the date of Yom HaShoah placed a remarkable legacy into it, words of a path of spiritual optimism sustained in the face of the most profound evil. Not only is the date set carefully proximate to draw attention to the seven hundred and fifty resistance fighters and the Warsaw Ghetto uprising, most Yom HaShoah services have two songs requested by the survivors that are prayers of faith and courage. Hirsch Glick, active in the Vilna Ghetto underground, is said to have written the original Yiddish lyrics of the Partisan's Song that became the hymn of the Jewish resistance against the Nazis. The translations that appear in the ritual guide below were developed with a cluster of survivors as we prepared just such a service.

RECIPE # 32
Creating
a Yom
HaShoah
Service

Yom HaShoah commemorations naturally tend to embody a respectful pluralism. This service generally has a character of simplicity, sadness, and dignity:

- Sing *Ani Maamin*, "I believe."
- Read or chant The Shoah Scroll.
- Watch a film or invite a speaker to recall the lives, ideas, ideals, and culture of those who perished.

- Pray the traditional Mourner's Kaddish or a form of it that incorporates the names of the concentration camps.
- Sing the Partisan's Song of resistance:

Ani Maamin

Ani Maamin
I believe
b'emunah sh'leymah
with complete faith
b'via-at ha mashiah
in the coming of a way out
ani ma-amin
I believe.
v'af al pi sheh-yitmah-may-ha
and even if it tarry
eem kol zeh ah-hah-keh lo
with all this I will await it
b'hol yom she-yavo
in every day that will come.

The Partisan's Song of Resistance

Refrain: Never say this is the final road for you,
Though leaden skies may cover over days of blue.
As the hour that we longed for is so near,
Our steps beat out the message—we are here!
Verse: From lands so green with palms to lands
    all white with snow,
We shall be coming with our anguish and our woe.
And where a spurt of our blood fell onto the earth,
There our courage and our spirit have rebirth.
Verse: The early morning sun will brighten up our day,
And yesterday with our foe will fade away.
But if the sun delays and in the east remains,
This song as password generations must retain.

The calendar cycle of Jewish life has forever been shifted by the addition of the second sacred cycle. We recall and mourn the Holocaust of our communities and families, and the six thousand who had barely survived only to die in Israel's War for Independence, and the remarkable rebirth of Judaism and our people through the restoration of our homeland and the revitalization of Judaism around the globe. An ancient people, we hold sacred not only the cycles of natural time—the seasons and phases of the cycles of human life—we also know time is linear, moving forward with difficult experiences and new ideas that can reshape the human future.

Even as we parade on Israel Independence Day,
our joy is shadowed by compassion and awareness
of other peoples' losses, needs, cultures, and hopes.

Our people has been the conduit of so many
gifts that have enhanced and advanced civilization
as the year turns past Tisha b'Av
the cycle of the year returns to *teshuvah*,
deep self-reflection and engagement with others
in service of healing relationships
rebirthing ourselves into another year.

We are a tender healing people,
Still praying for the kind of wisdom
that will lead to a universal peace.
May this come swiftly and in our time.

10

Rosh Hodesh and Kiddush Levanah
Revitalizing Natural Cycles

All the holy days we have studied thus far come but once a year. There are also, however, monthly practices and blessings keyed to the new moon and the full moon. In Judaism, the phases of the moon are seen as an inspiration to and the promise of renewal. The moon is feminine, and her phases are sometimes depicted as stages of pregnancy. In antiquity, women observed the new moon, Rosh Hodesh, as a day off from "labor" of all kinds. Men followed a full-moon practice called Kiddush Levanah.

But why was the moon so important? Sightings of the new moon were once critical to setting the clocks of many world cultures, including those of Judaism. Centuries before clocks and computers, the new moon in Israel was announced by using the light from campfires as beacons to be flashed from hilltop to hilltop.

And how did women get Rosh Hodesh as a day off? The practice is reported by scholars as early as the year 750 C.E., and is also recounted by Rashi, the famous French Torah scholar of the eleventh century, as well as by Talmud scholars called Tosafists in the twelfth to fourteenth centuries, and even by mystics in the eighteenth century. One gets the sense that women wanted this to remain a solidly supported practice, so they got it onto the books! Rosh Ḥodesh as a women's day off is reported in the midrash as being an eternal reward for and commemoration of the ethical valor of the biblical Israelite women who refused to give the men their jewelry to build the golden calf.

Kiddush Levanah is described in the Talmud as a day when Jewish men created burning tapers from sticks topped with flax. They would then ascend the hills around Jerusalem, each carrying his torch and bearing a palm bough for blessing the Source of Life on the occasion of the pregnant fullness of the moon. Really, I couldn't make this up.

The mystics observed the day before Rosh Ḥodesh as Yom Kippur Katan, a "little" Yom Kippur, using the darkness of the moon to sink into ethical self-reflection.

Today, Rosh Ḥodesh and Kiddush Levanah have become occasions for the renewal of intimacy during support group gatherings held on the phase of the moon appropriate for your gender. Right about here, men usually say to me, what would we get together and talk about?

RECIPE # 33
Moonshine
for Men:
Renewing
Your Power

Jewish men are beginning to rethink their roles, to ask what comes after patriarchy, to begin carving out meaningful roles without resorting to physical domination. Men have a lot to talk about. You have been treated as dispensable units of war by society, as economic beasts of burden, as unfeeling brutes. Jewish men have fallen prey to many other stereotypes as well, such as the expectation that each of them is capable of becoming a scholar, and the value that is placed on scholarship above all other pursuits. The pain engendered by these practices needs to be spoken, honored, and healed.

Sukkot is a great time for men to plan and hold their first Kiddush Levanah gathering, because Sukkot week always falls during the fullness of the moon. Here are a few talking points, although I'm sure you'll have lots to add to the list.

- To whom do you tell stories of the men who shaped you?
- Who are your current role models? Why?
- For whom do you serve as a role model, and how do you serve in that capacity?
- Name and describe the men whom you want to call *ancestor* and also those you may have shaken out of your family tree. Or, like Joseph in the Torah, who hid a silver cup in his youngest brother's saddlebag in an effort to repair a huge breach in family relations, is there someone you yearn to call back to you for another try?
- Will you bring your sons and nephews, the young men you mentor, into your men's circle?
- Will you bless them to shake their, ah . . . *lulav* . . . wisely?
- Will you share some secrets from your heart and listen to their questions, opinions, and stories?
- Do you know what is important and of concern to the young men in your midst? Listen; empathize

with how difficult it is to be a man today. Now is the time to honor those feelings, not to fix or deny them.

• Some men in your midst may be infertile, and that may be a matter of grief for them. Create space to hear their story, to honor their struggle.

• Some will be divorced, or in the midst of a marital breakup, entering a state not being addressed with any guidance in Judaism: how to live on your own, to love yourself, to feel whole and independent. What is the emerging men's wisdom on this subject?

• Some in your group will be gay men, few of whose stories are found in the sacred texts of Jewish tradition. Create sacred space and time to let the torah of such lives also be received as holy.

• And—it could happen—you might want to talk about women: for example, about how to love someone through the chaos of menopause. And it might feel quite good to have your Jewish men's group as a safe place to vent exasperation with other aspects of gender difference and gender competition. What are the frustrations of living in the midst of a gender-paradigm change?

• Some of you may have daughters. What is the role of a Jewish father with regard to his daughters? What do Jewish men desire for their daughters? What do daughters uniquely need from you?

• You might also want to talk about how to welcome women into the minyan in the synagogue and into the workplace while adjusting to the cultural shifts, the losses, and the many gains that have come from doing this.

- Listen to the timbre of your voices as you chant as men. This is a unique music. What adjectives might you use to describe it?
- Are there men you miss a lot—friends from school days, perhaps, or a mentor long gone? Call their memory into your circle; afterward, consider phoning those who are still alive.
- And is there a man in your life who never sat in such a setting with you, and oh, how you wish he had?

This model works nicely for either a Rosh Hodesh or a Kiddush Levanah group meeting:

RECIPE # 34
A Monthly
Model for
Women

- Many groups select two people who go around the circle with a pitcher of clear water, a towel, and a basin for a ritual handwashing during an opening *niggun,* "song without words."
- Next, the volunteer leader of the month introduces the theme she has selected with a short explanation, poem, text study, story, or teaching.
- A guided visualization can be helpful here to connect body and spirit to your thoughts on the subject.
- Now all members are invited to share their wisdom on the theme. Divide the available time by the number of those present and be sure to designate a gentle but firm timekeeper.
- About ten minutes before ending, hold a giant tallit aloft in the manner of a *huppah.* Invite those

who want blessings for healing to come under, and bless them. Invite those whose first time it is at such a gathering to come under, and have them say the *Sheheheyanu* prayer for new seasons of life.
- Conclude with the appropriate blessings, which can be found in most any siddur or prayer book.

Reb Goldie's Time Manifesto

Once normal to civilizations,
the observance of holy days
has become a radical, spiritual act of self-care.
Sacred time is shareware.
It's free.

The only condition is that you have to use it before you go,
there's no refund at the finish line.
Are you willing to say to employers, schools, partners,
and politicians:

"Today is set aside as holy,
not to be diluted by overdoses of work,
money matters, politics, homework,
telephone solicitations, television commercials.
This time is my birthright! You can't have it!"

And what if they say:
"Take ownership of your own time?
You can't have it!
We must use your life to feed our bottom line!"

Imagine yourself joining in leading the spiritual (r)evolution
with a response that might sound something like:

"Oh, no, I won't give all my precious time to you.
We Jews build beautiful, meaningful experiences in time.
We savor festival meals, engage in soul-refining rituals.

"In order to live consciously, we take time to reflect
and refine how we act,
how we live, how we love, and how we work.
I am writing the torah of my life with each lived day!
I want to ripen deliciously in the sun of life,
not race whipped to the finish line.

"I have every right to experience these Jewish
holidays in their deepest intentions:
nurturing my relationships,
celebrating the journey,
rejoicing in and respecting the power and
diversity of creation."

And if they say:
"No reason to think, no need to reflect.
Feel your feelings?
You look up at the stars and express the awe you feel?
You stop to question the ethics of your own actions?

"You say you're not coming in tomorrow
so you can sit with your children or friends in a *sukkah*
and meditate on the fragility of life, the beauty of nature!
You're late because you stopped to
say a memorial prayer for your parents?

"The work ethic is your spiritual model!
Our company is your family.
What's all this about freedom and Jews?"

And you'll say?

> Post your thoughts and questions about Jewish spiritual prac-
> tice for Reb Goldie at www.ReclaimingJudaism.org, this
> book's companion website. This site also offers Jewish spiritual
> practice discussion groups; online courses; information on
> Jewish spiritual teachers, workshops, retreats; and hundreds of
> free pages of additional guidance for deepening your under-
> standing, practice, and spiritual connection to Shabbat, holy
> days, life-cycle events, prayer, Torah study, peoplehood,
> Hebrew, mitzvot, and G*d.

PART TWO

Reclaiming the Sabbath

In the tapestry of the year,
the holidays can be seen as the woof,
changing the texture of time
with differing themes and practices.

The Sabbath, Shabbat, is the warp.
A weekly time warp,
reshaping time within the context of
blessing, holiness, and rest.

Judaism's most important practices
may prove to be gourmet items,
an "acquired taste"
for which your passion might grow.

Shabbat can be like that.
Perhaps you'll join me in saying,
"Why didn't anyone serve it this way
when I was growing up?"

SOLVING THE SABBATH MYSTERY

Shabbat is a treasure trove for those who are interested in reclaiming the spiritual practices of Judaism. Much of the juiciness of Sabbath practice was lost when our ancestors immigrated to new lands and began to focus on adapting to new cultures rather than preserving their own. Today, the obstacles to Shabbat practice are exponentially greater. In a society so dependent on speed that we upgrade our relatively new computers for a few nanoseconds' less response time, the very idea of taking an entire day off can seem like an impossible luxury. Even our children, according to a recent report issued by the National Institute of Child Health and Human Development, have four hours fewer to engage in unstructured play and outside activities per week than children had twenty years ago.

In some ways Shabbat is like an archeological dig, with hints of practices hidden by the mystics poking through the layers of time. There are levels to unveiling this mystery. Let's start at the beginning by noticing that what defines progress has become unclear. Is seeking ever-increasing profits and productivity the road to happiness or . . .

Slavery:
the inability to control the use of yourself
as a means of production

and the lack of ownership
of the right to organize your own time?
Are you the master of your own time?

Is anyone you know sick from stress?

Are there ways you enslave others,
forcing them to work late,
to work ever-longer hours
to bring home a living wage?
To what/whom are you feeling enslaved in your life?

Go ahead, make a list.

SHABBAT DISCOVERY #1: SHABBAT IS PART OF A HEALING PLAN FOR RECOVERING FROM SLAVERY

Shabbat practice requires explorations in the realm where myth informs consciousness. In order for the myth to touch in you what Jewish mystics call the Four Worlds—physical, emotional, intellectual, and spiritual—it will help if you temporarily suspend disbelief and be "in" the stories and their dramas.

Please turn your mind to the Exodus story. The Israelites have just fled a country where they'd been enslaved for generations. Having known no rest in their lives, they are weary and suffering from posttraumatic stress syndrome. Trained to follow orders, they yearn for self-rule and freedom. And, if they are to survive the vast wilderness journey ahead, they will need rest, healing, revitalization. From a G*d's-eye perspective, what can be done to begin their reeducation as free beings?

How does G*d relate to the Israelites' exhaustion? By comparing it to the experience of creating the universe. After six days and thirty-one verses of intense creative labor, we read in Genesis, *vah-y'hal*, "G*d finished the work that G*d had made." What might have been that finishing touch? What is something that is physical but not concrete? One possible clue is *va'yishbote*, "[G*d] rested." Rest was invented on the seventh day. At first glance not so dramatically visible as a mountain range or the heavens, yet so wonderful and astonishing that in the Torah G*d recalls the experience of rest as an "aha" moment that was more than "good" or "very good"; it became the first aspect of creation categorized as "holy."

Has your retelling of an experience ever tended to change over time? Maybe the first time you recall many of the details but are not so clear about the meaning of the experience. Then, sometime down the road, you find yourself reminded of that experience and discover that it means much more to you in retrospect. In fact, perhaps there was something significant and enduring about that experience that bears remembering and repeating. This is what happens in Exodus, where, while recollecting that first Shabbat at the end of the six days of creation, G*d describes it as a day of rest and *vah'yee nahfash*, "re-souling."

So let's go back to our exhausted Israelites and G*d in the role of concerned parent. A new cosmic "aha," worthy of shouting from a mountaintop, results from G*d's revisiting this seventh-day experience. Perhaps it went something like this:

Oh, people don't know about this, this method for revitalizing the soul! They imitate me by working ceaselessly, struggling endlessly. They don't know that labor and struggle without a regular concentrated time for restoration of their energy and spirit will destroy their bodies and souls and, ultimately, creation itself. I must share this memory as a teaching, guiding them to see "rest" as their first experience of holiness. What a perfect way to help my people!

SHABBAT DISCOVERY #2: PLAN TO LIVE EVERY SEVENTH DAY AS IF YOUR WORK WERE FINISHED

It would seem obvious, upon reflection, that the work of creating the universe was not finished in six days; in fact, it is nowhere near completion even now. We're looking at an ever-unfolding research and development project—new species emerging, worlds colliding in distant galaxies, endless change. You and I and everyone else are partners in the planning and completion of this never-ending project in the region assigned to us, which is, let's say, at least our solar system. So what happened on that seventh day? It seems that G*d invented rest and spent the day acting "as if" creation were finished. Could you do that? Live one day a week as if your work were finished?

In Exodus 16, before the Sabbath is engraved in stone as one of the top ten habits of highly successful humans, Moses conveys G*d's instruction to collect a two days' supply of manna and quail at once, in order to experience being free of this labor for a single day. Even so, conditioned to working ceaselessly, some do go out on the seventh day to gather food. Such a large helping of freedom proves difficult to trust, hard to swallow. The Israelites may have made it out of Egypt, but Egypt is still inside them.

To achieve personal change requires an additional step. The Torah account makes this clear: Sustainable change requires practice, a process of relearning in order to undo old patterns. This powerful medicine, weekly Shabbat practice, which was prescribed for the Israelites, is just as relevant for us.

RECIPE # 35
The Shabbos
Box

My teacher, Reb Zalman, once mentioned to me that his family had a Shabbos box wherein, just before the beginning of Shabbat, they deposited items requiring safekeeping until it was over. I imagine he meant such items as the keys to the office, wallets, messages to be returned. Today such a box would contain cell phones and PalmPilots, perhaps even television remote controls.

There is also a Shabbos box in your mind. Here is a practice that might help you to tolerate, even come to derive great *oneg Shabbat*, "Shabbat pleasure," from living as if your work were finished. (FYI, Shabbos, with the "s" on the end, is the Eastern European way of pronouncing Hebrew; since the founding of the State of Israel, Jews increasingly use the Sephardi pronunciation, which predominates today.)

- Close your eyes and, for about five minutes or more, count everything that registers in your mind: images, sounds, concepts, feelings, anything. Just notice each thought as it comes up; don't go into it in depth, just nod an acknowledgment to it, count it, and go on. (Examples: I didn't pay the health insurance bill, that's one; I really miss my best friend, two; I wish that cute guy in shipping would show some interest in me, three; oops, I didn't cook the green vegetable, four; and so on.)
- Tell all those thoughts that it's time to tuck them into the Shabbos box. Promise to return to them after Shabbat. Tell them: "If we give it a rest, you'll

see, I'll be refreshed and much better able to take care of your needs." Like children, such thoughts tend to get out of bed before their rest is completed and may need to be lovingly returned to their room and tucked back in.

• Whenever you have a thought or experience during Shabbat that could be useful for the workaday world, the goal is to consciously release it, to not hold onto the idea at all. Take the idea and place it on the altar of your intentions, sacrifice it in order to better *shamor v'zahor*, "honor and remember" Shabbat. When you do this, you are acting globally, taking part in "re-souling" civilization by slowing down and taking responsibility for doing what no one can do for you, the re-souling of your own self. This gift of time away from work will allow you to be far more present to significant others, to connect with community, cease laboring, and heal through celebration.

RECIPE # 36
The Mystery
of the
Seven-Branch
Menorah

Unlike the Hanukkah menorah, which has nine branches, the original menorah in the Temple had seven branches, one for each day of the week. The center branch of the original menorah is said to be Shabbat, those to one side are Wednesday, Thursday, and Friday, the days of anticipating Shabbat, and those to the other, Sunday, Monday, and Tuesday, the days when you still carry the healing light of Shabbat within you. You might try living for a week or two within this menorah model, making your Shabbat practice a stabilizing, harmonizing center for your week.

- On Wednesday, begin to anticipate Shabbat coming toward you in time. Find one thing of which you would love to let go. Be willing to make a commitment to step away from this labor that saps your energy rather than restoring your soul. All of Shabbat may be too long for you to do this, so perhaps a Friday night, or maybe just ten, fifteen minutes or a few hours, will be your planned getaway.
- Imagine how this respite will feel. In your body there may be a place where that toxic labor lodges. Imagine the light of the Shabbat candles coming into that sore place, soothing away your tension. Know that as Shabbat approaches you will be releasing that tension, creating a greater opening within you.
- Plan what you might do that will feel re-souling during the time you gain by practicing your commitment. Not so much something that would be fun or interesting, but rather something that will be soothing to your soul and fulfilling to you physically, emotionally, intellectually, and spiritually. You might create a palette of possibilities. Creative options will appear in the recipes that follow.
- On Thursday, begin any preparations that might be necessary to implement this two-faceted plan, and finish your preparation by Friday. (Examples: Inflate the air mattress to float in the pool; buy

toppings for ice cream to serve after Shabbat lunch; research the location of a nearby stream to walk to on Shabbat and see what can be learned from observing flowing waters; pick up a copy of the Torah to read a bit, and imagine what it felt like to be one of those characters.) Have your "retreat" planned and all your supplies at hand.

- Plan something to have on hand to end your Shabbat—a glass of wine, fragrant spices or flower petals, and a multiwicked havdalah candle are the traditional items.
- Shabbat arrives. Implement your plan.

> For Shabbat:
> What feels sensuous between your fingertips? Wear it.
> What is your favorite Jewish melody? Sing it.
> What helps you feel safe, snug, healthy, and home? Bring it.
> Which people sweeten time when with you? Invite them.

- Reenter the week. Are you time-shifted, a gentler, more centered being? Allow the flavor of your Shabbat to remain as a memory, influencing you. Notice how your body and your spirit feel. Did something subtle heal while you weren't concentrating on it?
- Somewhere around Wednesday, should your energy begin to wane, remember that it is only three days to Shabbat, your time of renewed re-souling. Perhaps you will choose to let the weeklong menorah practice begin anew. It is a tradition to begin wishing others a "good Shabbos" or "Shabbat

Shalom" starting on Wednesday! This helps create a shared sense of the peace and delight of Shabbat coming toward you. If you have forgotten the *Havdalah* closing ritual, it is also possible to offer it as late as Tuesday!

See how it feels
to make Shabbat
the center of your week,
rather than the end of it.

The mystics found
that Shabbat became
a central,
stabilizing,
harmonizing
pillar in life.

Without it, do you have one?

Your answer to this last question might have been that there is a pillar in your life already, perhaps a spouse, a parent, an employer, work, your art, the "state." But is it really fair or healthy to put others in such a position? Shabbat is a practice that helps you stay centered within yourself.

WHAT IS DEFINED AS WORK?

The Jewish people really discovered the stabilizing centrality of Shabbat practice when the Temple in Jerusalem was destroyed. That Temple had been the apparent central pillar of the community, organizing life into the comforting rhythms of a tribal-style culture. When the Temple was gone, the special sacrifices that had always been offered on Shabbat were no longer possible. Even so, through the pain of the loss and the trauma of exile, our hearts broke open and our souls flew up to a new level of spiritual development.

Shabbat practice, then as now, included cessation of constructive work. In fact, the thirty-nine categories of work that are forbidden on Shabbat are derived from the lists of Temple-building activities in the Torah. In addition to the lengthy list of assignments for building the new sanctuary that is provided in Exodus 31:13, there is also the requirement that all such work cease on the Sabbath. In contrast to when they were slaves laboring to construct the pyramids, the Israelites are delivered into a new model for living that includes self-care and rest in the form of a weekly sabbatical as a value for all beings.

To work on the Sabbath was to become cut off from your people. Those who worked when everyone else was resting, connecting, and celebrating creation lost the precious gift of concentrated time with community, family, and friends. When the Temple was destroyed, the curtain of its mystery was pulled back, the high priest brought out from behind it, and a simple person revealed, the ever-important *pintele Yid*, "individual Jew." Each tiny "point" of light that is a Jewish soul engaged in Shabbat practice acts as a high priest, sacrificing productivity to the essential process of re-souling a world that is endangered by always running full throttle.

By refraining from all the tasks involved in building the Temple, even in the absence of the physical Temple, you get to experience a spiritual temple, what the poet Hayyim Nachman Bialik, and later Rabbi Abraham Joshua Heschel, termed a "sanctuary in time." The original thirty-nine activities adopted as the practices to refrain from on the Sabbath are continuously being adapted to changing times and technologies. The original practices to avoid looked like this: the lighting of forge and altar fires, sewing the clothing of the priests, constructing walls, hauling materials, making furniture, and so on. After about two millennia, Shabbat practice has evolved to include a day of freedom from engaging in your particular occupation and labors such as cooking, shopping, travel, or intrusions from the outside world such as television, telephone, and e-mail.

There is a wide range of Sabbath practice among Jews. Some of us emphasize being *shomer Shabbat*, "guardians" of the Sabbath, keeping up a scrupulous guard against engaging in any of the proscribed activities. Others of us are more inclined toward being *zoher Shabbat*, creating lives rich in the spirit of Shabbat within more flexible parameters of observance. I like to imagine that, from a G*d's-eye perspective, together we do *dibur ehad*, "speak as one."

The Shabbat hymn *L'ha Dodi* speaks to this notion of a bouquet of diverse approaches to joyful Jewishing as we weekly sing, *"Shamor v'zahor v'dibur ehad"* (Guard and remember and speak as one).

PRODUCT WARNING LABEL

It is possible to destroy communal and family intimacy by losing a sense of balance between *keva*, "form," and *kavannah*, "intention." In exile it became customary to build fences around the core forms of Shabbat practice. One example would be the issue of whether instruments can be played on

Shabbat. In Temple times, instruments were a normal part of services. There are famous depictions of King David dancing and playing music on Shabbat. When the sanctuary-in-time concept began to evolve, however, the question arose: But what if a string breaks on your lute? Would not repairing it be work, a labor that would break Shabbat? From this question come variations in synagogue practice: Some allow instruments with the understanding that repairs won't be made on Shabbat while others eschew instruments entirely as a fence against the temptation of repair. The Talmud is full of Jewish sects formed as a result of subtle disagreements over how to practice Judaism. When differences in fences intended to protect core practices are seen as "offences" and become walls between communities, when Jews are unable to step into each other's worlds with respect, then the holiness and unity of our vision leeches out.

This also happens at the level of individual families, with equally traumatic results. A new and dear friend of mine who is reclaiming Judaism at the age of seventy recalls: "My childhood assignment to prepare for Shabbos was to tear the toilet paper into strips and place them in a box beside the toilet. I hated this lonely task that was always mine to do." We cried together at the impact on a child of associating Shabbat with toilet paper.

> When the container becomes more important
> than the contents,
> the spirit of Shabbat is lost.

My friend suffered more than fifty years of disconnection from the many aspects of Judaism she would have loved and lived—

peace, intimacy, relaxation, and opportunities for creative expression in song, dance, prayer, and dialogue. No one ever even explained to her the reason for her strange assignment: During Shabbat one generally tries to neither create nor destroy nor repair physical objects. Hence, before the advent of tissues, some pious Jews would tear sheets of toilet paper in advance to honor the spirit of Shabbat. Her family got so caught up in maintaining the fence that they never involved their daughter in the joys and mysteries of preparing for Shabbat.

This is not to say that cultivating fences around practices is inherently bad. When done collaboratively, with respect and space for the diversity of souls in a family, it can be a practice that is indeed *hiddur mitzvah*, adding to the "glory" of the mitzvah.

RECIPE # 37
Building a
Fence around
Shabbat

Shabbat is a vulnerable practice. Let's take the example of a stockbroker or someone in a relationship with a broker. Hearing the market report late on Friday afternoon, reading or watching the news on Shabbat, perhaps being asked a business question by a client you happen to see in the park during a Shabbat stroll might introduce trauma that would drain the healing out of your Shabbat. My broker friends who celebrate Shabbat have taken to avoiding media news sources just before and during Shabbat and letting their friends and clients know that they don't talk business or check their business line for messages on Shabbat. It has become their zealously protected weekly vacation.

How do you typically sabotage yourself
when it comes to getting time away from
things that tire, disturb, or distress you?
How would it be if you were to put down
the burdens you are carrying?
For ten minutes?
For an hour?
For one whole day?

How would it feel?

- What occupies you that will benefit from a rest?
Make a list. This won't necessarily be what we typically think of as work. An attorney friend who is
crocheting one hundred yarmulkes for her son's bar
mitzvah also has realized the value of ceasing from
this labor on Shabbat.
- Brainstorm several strategies, a.k.a. fences, to help
yourself not to engage in that activity or thought
pattern on Shabbat.
- Share your list with friends and anyone who lives
with you. Ask them to help you to pick one fence to
try out. You may add others later. Incremental adop-
tion of a practice works best, and, like signing up for
an exercise routine at the gym, a new practice usually
falls by the wayside when you take on too much too
soon. While others in your life may eventually join
you voluntarily, pushing them into a practice that
interests you usually backfires. Inviting their help in
your selection of a practice may reduce sabotage from
those who would otherwise not understand.

WHY GOVERNMENTS SUPPRESS SHABBAT

In the pre-perestroika Soviet Union, to be discovered practicing Judaism, observing Shabbat, or studying Torah was punishable by the loss of your job and imprisonment. It was a crime against the state. This was also the case in Maccabean times under the Seleucid Empire, and at many other points in history. What is so threatening about this practice that empires would seek to suppress it? Perhaps the breath of freedom, the spirit of intimacy, the glimpse of something truly great. How about a taste?

RECIPE # 38
A Taste of
Shabbat

This is a guided visualization that can be practiced alone and also read aloud during a group experience.

In a few days a favorite friend will arrive to stay with you for a night and one full day. This friend always brings out the best in you. Looking around, you come up with a list of ways to ready your home for welcoming your friend. You clear your calendar for the whole day. There are favorite things you will want to do together.

Dinner. Hmm. You begin to plan something special. You shop in advance for just the right wine, the perfect bread, and as a real treat, a seriously decadent dessert. As you shop, the pleasure this visit will give your guest occupies a warm, happy place in your thoughts.

Now, take the metaphor up to the next level: The guest is your beloved. Time changes when you are together; you feel different, more alive. When you're together you can't think of other things. Work doesn't matter, errands don't matter, just being together is everything. At the thought of your beloved, your soul leaps like a candle flame, dancing, flickering in anticipation: "My beloved will be here soon!"

And you want to look your best, to wear something your beloved will enjoy seeing. You pick a fabric that feels pleasurable against your skin and highlights the color of your eyes—special clothes that make you feel special.

All week you can feel your beloved coming toward you in time. No other days are like the ones when you're together. Other days seem so full of effort. When your beloved arrives, time is pure being. An ode to such love catches your eye; you save it to read when you are both together.

Your beloved is coming. This weekend, as the sun sets, you will be together. You want your family and friends to meet your beloved, and so you decide the dinner will be a party, a reception to welcome the light of your life.

Oh, but when your beloved has to leave, it is so bittersweet to let go, to return to the mundane rhythms of the week. Your time together has been magical; it is as though you were departing from the palace of a queen, leaving behind a time of sensuous living and sweet connection. Mourn not. Next week your beloved will come again, for your beloved is G*d wrapped in veils of time, wearing a garment of light. Her name is Shabbat.

The visualization is ended. Here is its source text:

Sunday had Monday, Tuesday had Wednesday, Thursday had Friday. Only Shabbat was left alone. The Sabbath came before the Holy One and said: "All the other days have a mate, am I to be without one?" The Holy One of Blessing said to it: "The Community of Israel shall be your mate." As it says in Exodus 20:8 'Remember the Sabbath day *l'kaddsho*,' 'to betroth it.'"
(Genesis Rabbah 11:8)

Should you engage in Shabbat practice, you may find, as I did while I was single, that a Jew who celebrates Shabbat is never alone. By the week's end your partner in time has arrived, you line your table with guests to greet the beloved, and no matter what transpired that week, you too will experience the mystery of being filled with Shabbat de-light. If you are in a committed relationship, Shabbat can also bring a special kind of healing for you. Here is a story that points to one way this might happen:

THE <u>H</u>ALLAH MEDITATION

A *fabrengen* is a <u>H</u>asidic storytelling form that can bring a group of people into a state of spiritual passion and deepened understanding of a particular point of practice. This example took place under unusual circumstances, in the Cabaret Club at the Nevele Resort Hotel in the Catskills during a seminary retreat. The original fable is adapted from a work by Rabbi Naomi Steinberg. My accomplice, Cantor Sol Zim, as fate would have it, is not only one of the preeminent cantors and Jewish composers of our time, he was once part of a famed Catskill cabaret act, the Brothers Zim.

> *Reb Goldie narrates:* Our story begins as a brilliant young rabbi, of growing renown for his ability to figure out complexities in the Torah, agrees to marry the daughter of the wealthiest family in town. As was the custom, her father would provide the new couple with a house and financial support so that they would never have to work for a living and the rabbi could continue to study and serve as a scholar for the rest of his life. The wedding, of course, was a joyous and elaborate affair.

Nearby, at the grand piano, Cantor Zim is softly chanting Jewish wedding blessings in the background. Then, on a swell of sweet music, he brings the audience into the singing of the joyous wedding song, "Siman Tov."

Yours Truly continues from center stage. But, as you might expect, their good fortune did not last long. (*A big stage sigh, please.*) The family business suffered a reversal of fortunes and the young scholar was informed that he would have to seek out a community in which he could work as a regular rabbi.

"OYYYYY," groaned my audience of rabbinical and cantorial students. "OYYYY," moaned the young rabbi, whose father had been a congregational rabbi. He knew this change would mean board meetings, congregational politics, supervising the Hebrew School, struggling with parents whose children never would have acted as their teachers reported. Being told no, no, not a fresh melody for one of the prayers at services; we love the old one! And all the other challenges many clergy experience in their pulpits, which result in less time for scholarship and a sapping of creative energy.

Cantor Zim leads a mournful verse from the Book of Lamentations: "By the waters of Babylon we laid down and we wept for thee, Zion." Sacrilege? No. Ask Shakespeare, tragicomedy works as a teaching tool.

Inquiries are sent out to find the best position for the young clergy couple. A wealthy man in a very rural area makes sure that his community provides the best offer. So they move to *Yenemsvelt* (Yiddish for *the middle of nowhere*), very distressed to give up the dream life they had always expected. (*Can you hear the violins?*)

The offer of support turns out to have certain limitations. Other than the rabbi's living expenses, there is really no budget for the little synagogue. The rabbi turns to his wife and informs her that even the <u>h</u>allah (sweet braided egg bread) for the *oneg*, a dessert reception after services, will have to be made by her. They can no longer afford bakery-bought ḥallah.

The rabbi labors very hard, and, not having a cantor or being at all musically inclined, leads a feverishly muttered service, then pauses and launches into his scholarly presentation on the weekly Torah portion. Now, *oneg* means "delight." Its Hebrew letters are the reverse of *nega*, meaning "plague." Friday night services are like a wedding. The tired beings who need to heal from being *nega*, plagued with the stresses of the week, are married to the bride of rest, which is Shabbat, and so the meal afterward is a type of wedding feast, called an *oneg*, a delight.

At the *oneg*, the rabbi's heart falls when he sees the two loaves of ḥallah his bride has made. They are *fabrent* (Yiddish for burnt),

> *farshimmelt* (tattered),
>> *seh'kruḥeneh* (wrinkled),
>>> *farfallen* (didn't rise right/a complete loss),

a mess!

We make a song of it: "fabrent, farshimmelt, seh'kruḥeneh, farfallen, a mess." It becomes a chant filling the room.

The rabbi's little rural community, however, doesn't seem to be put off by the hideous ḥallah. At the *oneg*, the *ha-motzi* blessing over bread is said, the ḥallah eaten. A festive evening with a special happiness begins to emerge.

At this point the senior citizens' group that is sharing the resort facilities has gone from peering in to sitting in. Cantor Zim now has everyone joyfully dancing around the Nevele Cabaret while singing his signature tunes of Sabbath celebration.

Word of the special Sabbath joy at the little synagogue spreads far and wide and the little shul (affectionate Yiddish term for a synagogue) is packed Sabbath after Sabbath. Proudly, the rabbi tells his bride: "We are doing so well here, you no longer have to make ḥallah for the synagogue. We can afford to buy ḥallah from the bakery once again!"

The next Shabbat, at the *oneg*, he gazes at the two gorgeous, glazed ḥallah breads as if they were trophies rewarded for the labor of his life. His heart is so full that he doesn't notice that the *oneg* lacks some of the joy of previous weeks.

Here Cantor Zim launches into the familiar cadence of Adon Olam, *a majestic hymn to the Eternal.*

The rabbi works harder and harder on his scholarly Torah teachings, amazed at the impact they seem to be having by the time of the *oneg* Shabbat. He doesn't notice the murmuring at services when he begins his talks or realize that bets have been placed on how many pages he will get through this week before Yankel, the retired rabbi who always sits in the second row, falls asleep.

"Az de rebbe shluft, und az de rebbe shluft . . . " The Yiddish song about the Ḥasidim *tiptoeing a dance while the rebbe sleeps begins to swell through the room, as if we all knew it had to be sung next.*

Attendance at services begins to dwindle noticeably, so the rabbi writes furiously, creating more and more elegantly reasoned, elaborate sermons. Finally, the day comes when he faces his bride and says, "Alas, my dear, you must once again begin to make the ḥallah yourself."

On Shabbat the rabbi looks at the bread, *fabrent, farshimmelt, seh'kruḥeneh, farfallen* . . . (feel free to join in) . . . a mess! Two memorial stones to his failure. It is all he can do to restore his Shabbat sensibility, and he is amazed to find the community spirit quite lively at the *oneg*. People look at one another as if to say, "Ah yes, this is how it was. This is why we come!"

The next Friday morning the rabbi sets aside his books, papers, and sermon writing, and enters the kitchen. "I am here to watch you bake ḥallah," he announces. His bride is quite flustered, aroused from her reflections before the bowl of rising dough: "What is there to watch? A little flour, some water and yeast, much patience during the rising, the meal to make, the twins to dress and myself; then some pounding, more rising, some baking. Feh, it almost makes itself!"

"No, there is more. I am sure." He sits back in his chair, puts his feet up on a bench, and declares, "Today you are the rabbi and I am the student." (*The audience softly cheers.*)

"Well, dear, you have missed the first phase. The dough is almost finished rising. Now one takes it and begins to raise the sparks of energy that give the ḥallah its life. Here I transform this plague of a week from *nega* into *oneg*, delight."

She gives a good punch, releasing all the air from the risen dough. "This pounding is for the hard time the congregation president gave you about the length of your teaching; this is for having to sell your favorite study table in order to buy clothes for the twins, who are growing so fast. This pounding is for how much I miss my family back home; and this is a prayer for all these disappointments that they might be transformed into ḥallah and do the world some good."

For the first time the rabbi holds his bride as she cries. Feeling his own tears and frustration rising, he lets them flow, too. Until then, he had seen only himself in the mirror of the ḥallah and never given a thought to the soul who made them.

Cantor Zim picks up the theme by singing a solo, a recitative to the purity of the soul, reborn, cleansed by preparations for Shabbat.

While one yet breathes, it is never too late to create a fresh new chapter in the scroll of your life. The *rebbetzin* continues. "Now we must create two sets of three strands, one for each ḥallah." She hands the rabbi some dough, motioning for him to divide it as instructed. She says: "These are the strands of my Shabbat meditation. As you probe and shape and activate the first strand, bring to mind everyone in the congregation who needs some guidance. Pray for them to see the great resources all around them, for all possible blessings to become visible to them. Pray they will receive what they need." Very slowly, side by side, they each probe and shape their first long strand of ḥallah.

"Now, on to the second strand. As you shape it, reflect on every person in the congregation who needs healing. See their faces, send a prayer to the Holy One of Blessing to notice them, to ease their suffering, and where possible to restore their vitality and renew their spirit." Here they help each other, one remembering the name of a woman who had just miscarried, the other a farmer with many young children whose leg was severed in a trap, and on and on. For the first time since moving to that town, the rabbi cries for his people.

"So, silly husband, look, you are getting tears in the ḥallah! No matter, a few tears will add to the holiness. The last strand is a meditation on gratitude. On this strand I recall with such thankfulness the great blessings that have come to some of the congregants this week. And when I look at you, all I see when I make ḥallah is that you are my beloved and the greatest blessing in my life. I pray for every single person in the congregation to find such a mensch, such a dedicated, good husband as I have." Then she takes a bit of dough and, in accordance with tradition, tosses it into the lower fiery furnace portion of the coal stove, intoning the ancient blessing for the "sacrifice" just made.

"What do we do now?" asks the rabbi.

"We braid the strands, bringing our community together in blessing. Then we gently cover the two loaves and wait for them to rise. Now, go back to your writing, I have children to dress." Instead, he takes her hand and pulls her closer, humming *L'ha Dodi*, as a waltz. *We all join in. Some commence gracefully waltzing in the aisles.*

Together they glaze the twin loaves with egg white and place them in the oven. And together they dress the children, now awake from their nap. The smell of burning brings everyone racing to the kitchen. As the rabbi removes the slightly overdone <u>h</u>allot, somewhat lumpy from the intensity of the prayer that has shaped them, he is laughing and laughing and declares at once to both his wife and the *farshimmelt* loaves: "Oh, how beautiful you are!"

Sol and I emerge from the trance-like state of leading the fabrengen. Perhaps inside each person in the room the <u>h</u>allah meditation will now live, like starter dough, for many a Shabbat to come.

RECIPE # 39
Your Role in
the Cosmic
Wedding

Removing the layers of *shmutz*, politics, and trauma that accrue during the week and rebirthing yourself into wholeness and a higher level of functioning with your friends and family can be greatly supported by the Kabbalists' model of Shabbat practice, engaging in the drama of the Royal Cosmic Wedding. This model shifts the focus of living away from the workday emphasis on how you choose to affect creation and onto practices that allow you to sense how much you are *affected by* the awesome processes that occur beyond your range of daily awareness. The effects of this form of Shabbat practice are many. Here are the basic secrets, some of which may be familiar, the sum of which may contain surprises:

SECRET #1: Genesis says that G*d *vah-y'<u>h</u>al* on the seventh day. This is usually read to mean that on the seventh day G*d "finished." But, the root <u>h</u>al or *kal* is also the root of *kallah*, "bride," and so a mystical reading of this is, "G*d made a bride of the seventh day." This interpretation is a primary source for the concept of the Cosmic Wedding.

SECRET #2: Your home is the *huppah* and the site of the wedding reception. That's why so much attention is paid to beautifying it with flowers and providing delicious meals.

SECRET #3: It is a white wedding. That's the source of the traditional use of white tablecloths, white candles, and, in some communities, wearing white clothing on Shabbat. In Judaism, white is the color of transformations of the soul; hence the color of a shroud is white, as are wedding dresses and circumcision layettes.

SECRET #4: Sensing the "bride" coming toward you from a distance, you long for her, the weekend, Shabbat, to arrive. You not only bathe physically, you also immerse yourself spiritually, seeking to loosen any *shmutz* that is clinging to your soul, blocking your readiness for this reunion.

SECRET #5: Poetry comes to your lips at the thought of "her." The Song of Songs is an allegory, a passionate Shabbat love poem read at this time of awaiting, expressing desire for unification, an end to exile, loneliness, distance. If partnered, you and your partner might take turns reading verses to one another, or, in a garden or beside a window, speak the words of this poem to Shabbat. The language is guaranteed to warm you up!

SECRET #6: Your beloved approaches veiled. At the beginning of Friday night services there are six psalms intended to help remove the veils of stress and effort from each day of the week, to lift any residue that might obstruct your ability to receive the bride. The bride is *Sheḥinah* consciousness, intimacy. The mystics spoke of your awareness of *Sheḥinah* as entering exile during the week and being restored to you when you open up time for intimacy through your Shabbat practice.

SECRET #7: One lights Shabbat candles eighteen minutes before sundown on Friday night. Just as Roman numerals are also letters, Hebrew numbers have numerical values, an *aleph* is one, *bet* is two, and so on. The word *ḥai* (often spelled *chai*), "life," is composed of the letters *ḥet*, with a value of eight, and *yud*, ten; so the number eighteen has come to be associated with the gift of life. Because Shabbat is about re-souling yourself, reenergizing, eighteen extra minutes of "life" are taken from the week and added to Shabbat.

SECRET #8: Shabbat begins with the lighting and blessing of at least two white candles, each representing a state of consciousness. One is *Sheḥinah* consciousness, the nurturing quality of spirit that comes through you, ideally to fill the activities of daily living with compassion and connection. *Sheḥinah* consciousness, your own and that of others, can wear thin and fragment during the week. The second candle is *Kodesh Baruḥ Hu* consciousness, remembering that you are part of a vast Eternal Flow of Being that is Becoming, the Big Picture, also called *Meleḥ*, "King," which is why, at this Cosmic Wedding, Shabbat is called a bride who will become a *Malka*, "Queen."

SECRET #9: The sacred phrase spoken before lighting the Shabbat candles and also before Shabbat lovemaking is about the desire to experience and dwell in the healing whole of unified consciousness: *L'shem yihud Kudsheh Brih Hu u'Shehinteh*, "For the sake of the unification of the Holy One Blessed be G*d and G*d's *Shehinah*."

SECRET #10: Who is in the wedding party? You and the guests around your Shabbat table, and, when you are in synagogue, the congregation. All escort the "bride" down the aisle by singing *L'ha Dodi*, "To You my Beloved," the seventh prayer in the Friday night service, following the six psalms that lift the veils from the face of the *Shehinah*.

SECRET #11: You are the bride. You are also one of the candles. The *Shehinah* consciousness radiating from within you continues down the aisle to the ark.

SECRET #12: The ark opens and the other aspect of Consciousness beyond and within you called *Meleh*, "King," is revealed. *Meleh* is represented by the Torah, wearing its silver crown(s). This king metaphor is used on Shabbat to represent the left brain, the analytical and intellectual qualities that await reunification with the right brain, the qualities of intimacy and emotion that are *Shehinah* consciousness.

SECRET #13: Singing the hymn known as *Shalom Aleihem*, "May peace and wholeness be yours," you invite angels, *mahlahei ha'shareyt*, to escort the bride into your home or synagogue, both of which serve as the *huppah* or "bridal canopy." Who are the angels? These are the other guests or congregants, and Jewish tradition, having traveled through medieval times, also has a large angelology with names like Azriel, Uriel, Gabriel, Raphael, among many others.

SECRET #14: When did you get engaged? After the Exodus from Egypt, as a member of the pool of all Jewish souls standing at Sinai.

SECRET #15: In the synagogue, the wedding continues as you bow for the *Baruḥ Hu* prayer, allowing the flow of spirit, as the mystics say, to pour over you when you arise so that you, too, are crowned like the Torah. *Your* crown, however, is the radiance of a bride, a *Sheḥinah* radiance, a crown of light.

SECRET #16: At every Jewish wedding, and so, too, at every Shabbat table, is a kiddush cup filled to the brim with red wine. Wine symbolizes *gevurah*, strength, blood rising with procreative energy and life force. Sipping it strengthens you for the Shabbat nuptials of body, mind, and spirit. The Kiddush or "holiness" prayer said over the wine on Shabbat represents the wedding vows, the actual moment of commitment. During synagogue services, we say a prayer whose opening words are based upon the words of the traditional wedding vows, *Atah Kidashtah*, "You are holy [unto me]."

SECRET #17: The Kiddush incorporates verses that recall the gifts received during the original commitment process of the Jewish people to our sense of G*d; those mentioned are creation, Shabbat itself, being brought out of Egypt, and the Torah.

SECRET #18: In the Kiddush you are singing that Shabbat comes from *ahavah u'v'ratzon*, "love and desire." It is a double mitzvah to make love on Shabbat and it is considered auspicious for procreation. Because in modern times many of us will be single for long periods, some contemporary sages, including my teacher Reb Zalman, counsel pleasuring yourself on Shabbat and offering up that wave of pleasure as part of your practice.

SECRET #19: Since you wouldn't be likely to work on your wedding day, you can luxuriate in the fullness of Shabbat. This open space in time becomes a womb for the *neshamah yeteirah*, the "extra measure of soul" that is said to arrive within you on Shabbat.

SECRET #20: What about wedding presents? These are the interpretations of the weekly Torah portion that you create and share in honor of Shabbat.

SECRET #21: What about the wedding reception? This is the *oneg*, "pleasure," provided in honor of Shabbat by foods intended to delight after services and on your Shabbat table. It is a mitzvah to prepare food in honor of Shabbat, so you need not hesitate to ask your guests to contribute a dish as part of their own practice.

SECRET #22: What about toasting the bride or the happy couple? The Shabbat service is rich in such prayers. At your home reception, it's customary to read the *Eyshet Ḥayil*, a poem praising the qualities of a fine Jewish wife. This practice can easily be gender-balanced by each partner's turning to the other and recalling special moments during which one or the other felt supported during the week. Children are traditionally blessed by their parents at this time as well. This practice can be similarly amplified by having the children recall special moments from the week when they felt supported by their parent(s) and blessing them, too!

SECRET #23: You can hold a good-bye party called a *melaveh malka,* "accompanying the queen," for Shabbat and her wedding guests in order to extend the Sabbath into the darkness of Saturday night. Traditionally you escort the Sabbath bride—and yourself—toward the week with wistful dance and song.

SECRET #24: Any time after you see three stars in the sky, or as late as sundown on Tuesday, you can do *havdalah,* the closing ritual for Shabbat that's explained in the following recipe.

RECIPE # 40
Letting Go
of Shabbat:
Havdalah
Practice

Ah, what a spiritual challenge it is to leave a restful Shabbat and reenter the week. Havdalah is the ritual designed to ease and sweeten that transition

- As at the end of a Jewish wedding, when Shabbat ends, the kiddush cup containing the symbol of the life force, red wine, is again taken in hand. This wine is symbolic of the flow of blessings throughout the day as well as the abundance of energy and joy that can be tapped into when you are well rested. Look how much has changed since you stood under the *huppah* with Shabbat just twenty-four hours ago! Let us bless, *borei p'ri hagafen*, "Creator of the fruit of the vine." Wait. Bless but don't drink. All sip from the cup of blessing at the end of the ritual.

- To ease the departure of your experience of *neshamah yeteirah*, "extra soul," fragrant spices are inhaled and their variety blessed. This is an olfactory memory aid you can call on for a spiritual lift during the week. Let us bless, *borei minei b'samim*, the "Creator of the varieties of spice" in life.

- The two stiff, individual white candles signifying that you and Shabbat had arrived to be present to each other are now replaced by a colorful, braided, multiwicked candle, its combined flame symbolizing your integration of consciousness, your increased energy for living, and the spiritual intimacy that has taken place this Shabbat.

- Kabbalists trim their nails before Shabbat. The white orbs that peek out from the base of each nail are a reminder of the *sitra aḥrah*, your "other [shadow] side." In the next step of this ceremony, many look at the candlelight reflecting in their nails, noting the lower white orbs, harbingers of the shadow side of life that manifests more easily in the work-a-day world. You can fold your fingers over to symbolize shielding your tender Shabbat-softened soul from the full force of the week to come. You might pray that, like the moon, symbol of *Sheḥinah* consciousness, you will enter the week as your best self, full of her reflected light. Let us bless, *borei m'orai ha eysh*, "Creator of the lights of the flame."

A final blessing is given, emphasizing the word-root meaning of havdalah, *l'havdil*, "to make distinctions," to recognize what is holy and what is not yet holy about the ways we live and love, and to bless the Source of this human ability.

Is it enough to enter the week as just pure humans? A touch of prophetic support is called for, a bit of messianic consciousness that among us are those who can help us all evolve toward peace, kindness, and successful coexistence. This help is invoked by singing a traditional hymn inviting support from the spirit of the prophet Elijah and, more recently, versions dedicated to the prophetess Miriam. In Jewish folklore, Elijah often functions as a family counselor and peacemaker. In Torah, Miriam could find water, the symbol of loving-kindness, an essential fluid of life, wherever she went.

To learn more, visit the expanded resource site for this book, located at www.ReclaimingJudaism.org: Post your thoughts and questions about Jewish spiritual practice,   find discussion groups; courses; information on Jewish spiritual teachers, workshops, retreats; expanded bibliography and hundreds of free pages of additional guidance for deepening your understanding, practice, and spiritual connection to Shabbat, holy days, life cycle events, prayer, Torah study, peoplehood, Hebrew, mitzvot, and G*d.

GLOSSARY

Note: Transliterations do not follow a formal, academic system; they are simply designed to facilitate ease of pronunciation. When two pronunciations are offered, the first is the modern Hebrew form and the second is an Ashkenazi (Eastern European) pronunciation still in use.

Adon Olam (ah-doen oh-lahm): Threshold of Eternity, often translated as "Lord of the Universe"; an amazing daily prayer acknowledging G*d as the force and energy that existed before creation of our universe and that will remain after our corner of the cosmos is gone.

afikomen (ah-fee-koe-men): Transliteration of a Greek term used for the matzah that is broken in half and then hidden during the Passover seder ritual and that must be found as the *epikomion*, "concluding revelry" in the Greek symposium upon which the seder was originally modeled. Symbolizes how what started as the *lehem oni*, "bread of suffering," becomes the bread of transformation, as we grow from reflection upon our people's and our personal and contemporary challenges to freedom. Children are usually the ones to do the searching, for the future depends on their joyful and meaningful involvement.

ahavah (ah-hah-vah): Love. A core principle in Judaism is to infuse love into one's actions and to draw inspiration from experiencing the greatest view of reality as one created out of *ahavah v'ratzon*, love and desire, as the Kiddush prayer describes.

ahsteer (ah-steer): "I will hide." A phrase in the Purim story of Esther understood to reveal the presence of G*d in a story that does not appear to mention G*d. This understanding encourages one to feel G*d within oneself as an inspiration to, like Esther, take action for justice under difficult circumstance.

Akedah (ah-kay-dah): Term for the intense scene in Torah where Abraham appears to be about to sacrifice his son.

aliyah, aliyot (pl.) (ah-lee-yah, ah-lee-yote): "Going up"; the act of a committed Jew done by moving to Israel, termed "making *aliyah*," going up to Israel, as Moses went up to Sinai, and the local parallel, going up to the Torah to witness it being read.

ameyn, amen (ah-meyn, au-mane): Amen. Root of *emunah*, "faith." It is also an acronym for *El meleh ne-ehman*, meaning: G*d is a faithful governing principle. "One who answers amen with all one's strength merits to have the gates of the Garden of Eden open before him" (*Shabbat* 119b). Also see *meleh*.

Ani Ma-Amin (ah-nee mah-ah-min): "I believe." Prayer of belief in redemption that became very important to many during the Holocaust.

Antiochus V (ahn-tea-oh-kuss the fifth): Governed the Greek-occupied cities of Syria from 164 to 162 B.C.E. He ascended the throne at age nine, and was known for corruption and failed efforts to put down a Jewish uprising that appears in the Purim story.

Aramaic (ar-uh-may-ic): A semitic language spoken by most Jews during the original developmental period of the Talmud. Also appears in many Jewish mystical writings such as the Zohar, and some traditional prayers, such as the Kaddish.

aravot (ah-rah-vote; in Ashkenazi, ah-rah-vose): Willow sprigs; one of the four species brought together in a Sukkot prayer ritual. Willow has neither fragrance nor taste and is said to represent the open valance of a soul that has not yet engaged in study and practice of mitzvot. Its leaves are shaped like lips and some teach this is a reminder to engage in ethical speaking practices as a way of fostering healthy community relationships.

ashamnu (ah-shahm-nu): We are culpable. Most often heard as part of a High Holy Day prayer sequence of taking responsibility for the marks one has missed in the year; the first step toward transformation is awareness.

assiyah (ah-see-yah): One of the four kabbalistic dimensions of spiritual practice; *assiyah* concerns the importance of attention to physicality, logistics, and grounding.

atzilut (ah-tzee-lute): Transcendent dimension of the four aspects of spiritual practice found within Hasidic and Kabbalistic traditions. This is where you connect beyond the known or conceivable and experience pure, unified Being.

aveyrah (ah-vey-ruh): To have committed an *aveyrah* is to have transgressed a negative commandment, such as in bearing false witness about someone.

bayit katan (bah-yeet kah-tahn): Literally "little house"; one's home is considered to be a temple in Judaism, a sacred space meant to be lived in with that consciousness.

B.C.E.: Acronym for "before the Common Era." Non-religious format designating years before the first century of our side of the timeline.

bedikat ḥametz (b'dee-kaht ḥah-meytz): Checking for and removing *ḥametz*, bread residue, in one's home is a ritual of symbolic purification of your living space from the bondage of your regular diet and other life practices that can interrupt your relationships and space.

beriyah (bree-yah): One of the four dimensions of spiritual practice offered by Kabbalists; this one concerns ideas, thoughts, and innovations.

beyn hameytzarim (beyn hah-mey-tzah-rim): "Between the straits"; describes the spiritual quality of the weeks between the ending breach of the walls at the siege of Jerusalem and the Tisha b'Av memorial day for those slaughtered and exiled and the destruction of the Temple and its way of life.

borei minei b'samim (boe-ray mee-nay b'sah-mim): "Creator of the varieties of spice"; from the Havdalah blessing, one of the ways of experiencing G*d.

borei m'orai ha eysh (boe-ray m'oh-ray hah eysh): Creation of the flames of fire; from the Havdalah blessing, one of the ways of experiencing G*d.

borei p'ri ha gafen (boe-ray p'ree- hah gah-fehn): Creator of the fruit of the vine; from the Shabbat opening and ending blessing, one of the ways of experiencing G*d.

Chmielnicki, Bogdan (ḥmel-nikki): A sixteenth-century anti-Semitic leader of an unsuccessful Ukrainian revolution that included his inciting the Cossacks to slaughter over one hundred thousand Jews.

C.E.: Common Era, which is the Jewish term for designating years starting in the first century of our side of the timeline, since AD is a Latin term referring to the Christian idea of time restarting in the Anno (year of) Domini ([their] Lord).

cholent (choh-lent): Jewish ethnic dish involving either beans or flanken, a cut of beef that can be set to cook before the Sabbath begins and left on a warming pan called a *bleh* throughout the Sabbath, to free oneself from cooking on the Sabbath.

Cohanim (coe-hah-nihm): Priests who served in Temple times; those who derive their lineage from them are called up to bless the community and to have the first *aliyah* to the Torah in some communities.

din (dihn): Law, judgment; in mystical sources the aspect of our nature that must be in balance with *hesed*, loving-kindness. In pictures of the Temple of Jerusalem and of the Tree of Life, one of the columns/pillars/channels of G*d energy is known as *din*.

dreidel (drey-dl): Four-sided top, with a Hebrew letter on each side representing the words: *nes gadol haya sham*, a great miracle happened there (and in Israel, *po*, "here"). It is spun on Hanukkah to remember how this game would be played when Roman guards were nearby to deflect them from realizing forbidden Torah study was taking place.

ehyeh (eh-yeh): The name G*d self-describes at the burning bush, meaning "I will be" or "I am becoming."

Eihah (ey-hah): Literally, "How?!" The first anguished word of the Book of Lamentations, the sacred text that recounts the slaughter and exile of the Jews by the Babylonian conquerors of Israel.

Elohim (eh-loe-him): One of the many names for G*d in the Torah; is regional G*d name "El" given in a plural form; some say this reveals the progression from polytheism to monotheism. In Jewish mysticism this term refers to how G*d manifests within the physical laws of our universe.

Elul (eh-lool): Name of lunar month that precedes the High Holy Days; traditional time to engage in practices of life review and *teshuvah*, attention to healing of relationships.

etrog (eh-trog, es-rug): Citron; one of the four plant species brought together in a Sukkot blessing ritual. This lemon-like fruit has both flavor and remarkable fragrance and is said to symbolize female fertility and also one who balances the learning and doing of mitzvot. Some see it as heart-shaped, pointing to the importance of inclining your heart toward good for all.

Eyshet Hayil (ey-sheht hah-yl, eyshes ha-yl): Ode sung at Shabbat dinner to a female spouse, honoring the valor of all her good works and concerns. Increasingly, complementary pieces for male partners are being created and recited as well.

fabrengen (fah-brehn-gehn): Hasidic story-telling method of intertwining passionate song and sometimes dance with an elegantly designed Torah-teaching so that the learning happens with greater ease and joy.

fabrent (fah-brent): Yiddish for burnt, as in food or emotionally, or one's personality.

farshimmelt (fahr-shih-mult): Yiddish for a rumpled appearance.

ganseh (gahn-suh): Yiddish for "entire," as in, "He told me the *ganseh megillah*," the whole story; implying even more details than hoped for.

geniza (g'nee-zah): Repository in which physically worn-out texts and scrolls that contain the *Shem Havayah*, YHVH—four-letter name of G*d—are put to rest.

gevurah (g'vooruh): Strength; symbolized by wine, and also is one of the ten sephirotic qualities of the Kabbalists' Tree of Life model. *Gevurah* practice concerns focusing on the quality and health of your personal boundaries and strength.

gragger (grah-gr): Noisemaking device of various types used to drown out the name of the villain in the Purim story-telling ritual.

haddas, haddassim (pl.) (hadas, hah-dah-sim): Myrtle; one of the four plant species brought together in a daily Sukkot prayer ritual. Myrtle has fragrance and its leaves are eye-shaped. It is said to represent one who is alert to and active in mitzvot, although unlearned. It is the root word for the Hebrew name of Queen Esther, Hadassah.

Haggadah, haggadot (pl.) (hah-gah-dah, hah-gah-dote): Ritual booklet for home-based Passover rituals. From *l'hageed*, "to tell."

hag habikurim (hahg ha-bee-koor-ihm): Festival of the First Fruits, biblical term for Shavuot.

hahnassat orhim (hah-nah-saht ohr-him): Phrase denoting the mitzvah of using best practices for receiving guests.

hai, hayyim (pl.) (high, high-ihm): Life.

halahah; halahot (pl.) (hah-lah-hah, hah-lah-hote): Term for Jewish law; also means walk, way, path.

hallah, hallot (pl.) (hah-lah, hah-lote; folk: hallie): Dough offerings that were brought to the Temple by the Israelites to help feed the busy priests and their families. This practice is remembered by serving a much-loved egg bread that is braided for the Sabbath and served as a spiral on festivals, suggesting the spiral of life and personal growth. Two *hallot* (pl.) are served on Shabbat to recall the double portion of manna harvested for Shabbat when the Israelites were in the wilderness. So too, Shabbat practice brings an extra measure of soulful vitality.

Hallel (hah-lehl): Festival service section of psalm singing.

hamas (hah-mahs): Origin of the term found in Lamentations and usurped politically today; is in the story of Noah and the flood where it means all-encompassing violence, total devastation.

hametz (hah-metz, huh-muhtz): Foods that were prepared before a facility was made kosher for Passover or that contain leavening or other products not considered kosher for Passover in one's particular community of reference.

ha-motzi (hah-moe-tzee): "Who brings forth." Core of blessing said at meals where bread is served.

haroset (ha-roe-set): Mixture of fruits and nuts for the Passover seder ritual that represents the mortar the Israelites were required to use as slave brick-layers for the ancient Egyptians.

havdalah (hav-dah-lah): Distinction, difference. Beautiful, brief ritual with wine, a lit braided candle, spices, and blessings for noting the end of Shabbat and the entry into a new work week.

havurah (hah-vue-rah): A group that tends not to be a full-service synagogue, but rather organized for a more limited subset of purposes such as joyful prayer, supportive community, and/or meaningful study.

Hellenism (heh-lehn-izm): Term for cultural practices prevalent during and spread by the Greek empire.

heshbon hanefesh (hesh-bone ha-neh-fesh): *Heshbon* means bill, tab, or account due, as in at a restaurant or a store, or in the story of one's life. This phrase refers to an accounting of the soul, *nefesh*, done on Thursday nights and on *Yom Kippur Katan* (day before each new moon), so as to be clear on what matters can be addressed now and which one can commit to attend to after Shabbat and Rosh Ḥodesh. This practice is also undertaken with great intensity throughout the month of Elul prior to the High Holy Days.

ḥevrutah (ḥehv-roo-tuh): Sacred study with a *ḥaver*, "friend."

heyt (ḥeyt): Archery term meaning to "miss the mark," often mistranslated as sin, given that Judaism views us as keeping ethical targets in sight, but being human, we will sometimes miss them and need to take note of this and refine ourselves to do better in the future. Remember, Torah is also an archery term, guidance for taking aim (with one's life).

hiddur mitzvah (hee-door meetz-vah): To "embroider" a mitzvah by beautifying the doing of it in some way is also a mitzvah!

ḥutzpah (ḥutz-puh): Yiddish for the quality of having extreme audacity.

Kaddish (kah-dish): Aramaic prayer which takes various forms, including a memorial for teachers and another recited by mourners; serves as an energetic bridge of G*d connection between each section of the three major daily services.

Kadosh Baruḥ Hu (kah-doesh bah-ruḥ hu, Hebrew): *Kudsheh briḥ hu* (Aramaic); Holy One, blessed be He. Traditional formulation of respectful speaking about G*d; *haShem*, "the name," is also used to refer to the most sacred name of G*d, YHVH, composed of all tenses of the verb "to be."

kallah (kah-lah, kah-luh): Bride. Affectionate term for the radiant feeling of the arrival of Shabbat.

kasher (kah-sher): Term for the processes of preparing a facility so that kosher food can be prepared in it; *kasher* is also used to refer to the draining of blood from meat before cooking, since Jews cannot ever consume blood.

katan (kah-tahn): Small, as in a *tallit katan*, a lightweight undergarment that has knotted fringes on each corner to remind one to live a mitzvah-centered life; first given at age three and worn by many pious persons throughout life.

kavannah (kah-vah-nah, k'vuh-nuh): Intention one brings to an action or practice; sometimes the term for a contemplative reading given to help one experience an aspect of prayer or to prepare for a mitzvah.

keva (keh-vah): Form, or fixed. The structure of a Jewish practice is often contrasted with the importance of the *kavannah*, "intention" one has when applying it.

kiddush (key-doosh): Prayer wherein G*d is blessed as Creator of the fruit of the vine on Shabbat and festivals, as a way of honoring and rejoicing in the Life Force within us all. Root word is *kodesh*, "holy."

Kiddush Levanah (kee-doosh l'vah-nah): Celebration of the full moon; a ceremony more recently engaged in as a men's and boys' night out for ritual and dialogue, since Rosh Hodesh has become a women's and girls' night out during the new moon of each month.

kitniot (kit-nee-ote): Category of beans and rice eaten by Sephardi Jews and many vegetarians but not those who are of Ashkenazi origin who eat meat.

kittel (kih-tl): Shroud. Soft white garments in which a deceased Jewish person is dressed by the *hevra kaddishah*, volunteer corps who recite psalms while gently washing and dressing the body for burial. The top layer of this layette is a white robe that some wear during marriage and on Yom Kippur to signify the process underway even then, which is the rebirth of the soul to a new dimension of being.

klal Yisrael (k'lal yis-rah-el): Literally, "all of Israel," meaning the Jewish people, everywhere we dwell, and the principle that we must care for one another, for history has shown we can only rely on ourselves for this.

klippah, klippot (pl.) (k'lee-pah, k'lee-pote): Literally, "shards, husks." Refers to protective emotional coverings you have within that develop via trauma and to the G*d sparks that are hidden under damage from the original big bang of creation that Kabbalistic practice teaches us to seek out and redeem through mitzvah-centered living.

kodesh (koe-desh): Holy. A quality of being or intention that shows great reverence for life and invokes awe. Same root as *kiddush* and *kaddish*.

Kohelet (koe-heh-let): Jewish term for the Book of Ecclesiastes; title is from the first word of the text, root form is *kahal*, assembly; a *kohelet* would be a speaker to those assembled to listen. The speaker in this text harvests pearls of wisdom and feeling from his elders and the text is traditionally studied on each Shabbat of Sukkot.

korban (kohr-bahn): Burnt sacrifice; from the root term *k'rav*, to draw closer; once done by burning the fat and entrails of animals (the priests and their families lived on the actual meat); points to a post-sacrificial system understanding of how unio-mystica comes about through the arousal of one's purest energies.

kugel (kuh-gl, or kih-gl): Jewish ethnic pudding made of noodles or potatoes with eggs and spices, sometimes with fruit and/or cottage-style cheese.

la'asok b'divrei Torah (lah-ah-sok b'dihv-ray toh-rah): To be immersed or occupied with words or matters of Torah; core blessing phrase for beginning a sacred text study session.

Lag b'Omer (log b'oh-mehr): Festive thirty-third day of the *Omer* period on which the anniversary of the death of the great mystic Rabbi Shimon bar Yohai is observed with bonfires. Some people also hold a ritual first-shearing of the hair of those around three years of age. Until this point in the *Omer* process, no joyous occasions are held; now the energy of sacred time shifts to welcome such occasions and they begin to proliferate.

latkes (laht-ks, folk pronunciation laht-keys): Potato pancakes, one of the traditional Hanukkah foods because they are cooked in oil. A popular Hanukkah story of late origin involves a tiny flask of oil said to miraculously last one week so that the Temple could be rededicated after it had been reclaimed from conquerors.

L'ha Dodi (l'hah doe-dee): Shabbat poem which invokes the spirit of Shabbat as a welcome, radiant bride.

l'hithaleh (l'hit-hah-leh): To walk. Same root letters as *halahah*, term for Jewish law meaning pathway or way to walk in life. Several characters in the Torah are said to walk with or before G*d, denoting a spiritual state of connection and awareness. The word is reflexive, indicating one walks one's self, i.e., walking with intention.

lifnei (lihf-ney): In front of, also literally, "before the face of."

lifsoah (leef-so-ah): Leap over; same root as *Pesah*, Passover.

lulav (loo-lahv): Palm branch, one of the four plant species held together in a Sukkot ritual; among the various symbolisms given to it are the spine, male fertility, and the scholar who is learned but undistinguished by good deeds.

maggid (mah-geed, mah-gihd): Jewish storyteller; shares the root of *l'hagid*, "to tell."

mahzor (mah-zore, mah-zr): Term for High Holy Day prayer book.

malah (mah-lah): Messenger, angel. Intriguing double meaning of this word allows for many spiritually interpretive opportunities, for who knows when someone in your life is one or both?

maror (mah-roar): Bitter herbs used as a symbol on the seder plate; it is also eaten with matzah to remind us of the bitterness of one who is enslaved.

mashiah, moshiah (mah-shee-ah, moe-shee-ah): Messiah. In Judaism this was first a term for a military leader who would succeed at bringing the remnant of post-exilic Jews back to sovereignty in Israel. Later became a term for one who would bring an end to human suffering. It has now been transformed in many contemporary Jewish circles to mean the ability within each person to contribute to a peaceful future for all.

matzah, matzot (pl) (mah-tzuh, mah-tzote): Flour and water, in contact for no more than eighteen minutes, rolled out, perforated (so that it will stay flat) and baked most often in a hot stone-based oven while chanting *l'shem mitzvah matzah*, "for the sake of fulfilling the mitzvah of making matzah."

matzah brei (mah-tzuh brai): Passover breakfast delight of matzah briefly wetted, mixed with beaten egg, a bit of pepper and salt, quickly fried, and then lightly topped with cinnamon-sugar, or maple syrup or jelly.

megillah, megillat (pl.) (meh-gee-lah, meh-gee-laht): Scroll, as in *Megillat Esther,* the Scroll of Esther. Also colloquial use as all the details of an event, e.g., "she told us the whole *megillah.*"

melaveh malka (m'lah-vuh mal-kah): Literally, "accompanying the queen." A program of sweet song to extend Shabbat on Saturday night rather than release the experience until the following week.

meleh (meh-leh): Literally "king." Often used to refer to G*d as the governing principle of the universe.

menorah (m'noe-rah): Candelabra used on Hanukkah to symbolize the one that once stood in the Temple in Jerusalem.

mensch (mehn-ch): Yiddish for an ethical person who one knows tends to do the right thing.

mezuzah, mezuzot (m'zoo'zah, m'zoo-zote): Small calligraphic scroll of verses from Torah placed into a protective case and set on all door posts except for the bathroom in one's home and office. Serves as a consciousness shifting tool so that every doorway becomes a reminder to fulfill what the scroll inside suggests, to make a difference by entering each room *shema,* "listening" and *v'ahavata,* "loving."

midrash (mih-drahsh): In every generation we find white space in our sacred texts to expand upon the meaning by creating stories about the characters and events that convey the intersection of our times and experiences with Torah.

mikvah, mikveh (mihk-vuh): Specially designed facility or naturally occurring body of living waters (ocean, lake, river) in which full immersion is possible for rituals of release, which help a soul engage in readiness for profound changes such as healing, marriage, lovemaking, conversion, and soul-level readiness for Shabbat and holy days.

minyan (mihn-yahn): Quorum of ten required to begin a religious service. Also assigned, in this book, to depict the inner and most committed family and friendship circle of a person's life.

mitzrayim (meets-rah-yihm): Egypt. Root word is *maytzar*, meaning "strait" and "birth canal"; serves as a metaphor in Torah, Psalms, and Jewish mystical interpretations of liturgy for being in a narrow place of oppression or constriction in one's individual or national life.

mitzvah, mitzvot (pl.) (mitz-vah, meets-vote): Often translated as "commandment," refers to sacred acts to be done with consciousness; 613 types are given in the Torah.

nefesh (neh-fesh): One of five terms for the soul.

neshamah (n'shah-mah, n'shuh-meh): One of five terms for the soul.

neshamah yeteirah (n'shah-mah y'tey-rah): Extra soul. Spacious Shabbat practice helps one give birth to an extra measure of soul.

niggun (nee-goon, nih-gn): Hasidic style of wordless melody that opens the soul to yearning, joy, and connection.

norah (noh-rah): Awesome and, by nature of that awesomeness, also terrifying and beyond our ability to fully grasp and certainly beyond our ability to control.

nusah (noo-sah): Each holy day and service has a particular melody tradition that quickly conveys to the educated participant which holy day it is and whether it is the evening, morning, or afternoon service.

oneg (oh-nehg): Pleasure. Term for a reception after Shabbat or festival services given for the pleasure of the guests and in honor of the holy day.

or ganuz (ohr gah-nooz): Hidden residue of the original light of creation that can be accessed via menorah practice for a healthier, holier future.

orlah (ohr-lah): Term for allowing a tree to grow for three years before eating of its fruit; given as the basis for not cutting a child's hair before age three.

Orpah (ohr-pah): In the Book of Ruth, she has a sister, Orpah, who elects to remain in Moab and not go with Naomi and Ruth to Judah after the death of their husbands.

pasul (pah-sul): Describes a scroll that is not in kosher condition.

pintele Yid (pin-tell-uh yihd): Affectionate term for being a Jewish soul; implies humility and simplicity of being.

Pirkei Avot (peer-kay ah-vote): The Talmud is based on an earlier text known as the Mishnah, and *Pirkei Avot* (often called Ethics of the Fathers) is one of the most widely studied sections of the Mishnah, perhaps because it is a collection of aphorisms for living that are depicted as stretching in time from Sinai to the time of Judah the Prince, editor of the Mishnah. It is customarily studied during the Shabbat afternoon meal, *Seudah Shlishit,* and also during the six Sabbaths of the *Omer* process.

pitom (pee-tome): The stem of an *etrog* that must be there for it to be kosher for use; can be viewed as symbolizing an umbilical cord, the vital connection of all life forms to each other through the energy of All Being.

rey'ah hah'nee-ho'ah (rey-ah hah-nee-ho'ah): Biblical phrase for a pleasing fragrance caused by the barbecue smell of a sacrifical offering.

seder, sedarim (pl.) (seh-der, say-dr; seh-darim): Literally, "order." Also the term for the heavily symbolic meal-based rituals of Passover and Tu Bi-Shevat.

Sefat Emet (s'faht eh-met, s'fas ehmes): Name for the Hasidic sage Rabbi Yehuda Leib Alter of Ger.

seli<u>h</u>ot (s'lee-<u>h</u>ote): Forgiveness prayers; also a service held ten days before Yom Kippur, late at night, in accordance with the mystics' experience that there is a *tikkun hatzot*, a "repair," that is possible in the dark night of the soul before dawn. Characteristic of the spirit of *Seli<u>h</u>ot* is Psalm 130: "Out of the depths I call to You; hear my cry, heed my plea . . . Who could endure it . . . if you kept count of every mark-missed? But there is forgiveness with You; therefore we are in awe."

sephirah, sephirot (pl.) (s'fear-ah, s'fee-rote): In the Kabbalists' holographic model for reality-mapping, they posit clusters of energetic qualities within a person and All-Being, e.g., loving-kindness, strength, compassion, and more. Each of these ten points is termed a *sephirah*, meaning sapphire and sphere.

seudat hamashia<u>h</u> (s'oo-daht hah-mah-she-a<u>h</u>): "Feast of the Messiah," a Hasidic practice for the last night of Passover in hope of the coming of a messianic-quality to the future. This practice is being adapted in other parts of the Jewish spectrum as well.

Shabbat, Shabbos (shah-baht, shah-bus): The Sabbath, one day out of seven dedicated to renewal, prayer, inspiration from Torah teachings, delicious meals with family and friends, lovemaking with one's partner, and the absence of workday stresses and obligations.

shalem (shah-lehm): Wholeness, completeness; same root structure as *shalom*, peace, and found in the Hebrew for Jerusalem, *yerushalayim*, "city of peace/wholeness."

shalom alei<u>h</u>em (shah-lome ah-lay-<u>h</u>em): Peace be upon you. Traditional blessing given when greeting others; also the title of a Shabbat prayer often sung at home after lighting the Shabbat candles.

shamash, shamos (shah-mahsh, shah-muhs): Extra candle on the menorah that serves to light the other candles; also the name for the caretaker role in a minyan or synagogue.

shamor (shah-more): To observe Jewish practices, like Shabbat.

sheheheyanu (sheh-heh-hee-yah-noo): Based on the root *heye* for being or existing; refers to the prayer spoken at many festivals and life-cycle events showing gratitude for having the gift of being alive to witness this *z'man*, remarkable interval of time with unique experiences of being blessed.

Shehinah (shuh-hee-nah): Name for G*d as intimately present, from the root *shahan*, "dwell." Is also a term for Shabbat.

shema (sh'mah): Listen! Spoken by Moses to get the Israelites' attention in the wilderness. His words became the central prayer in Judaism which asks us to listen, become aware, and live from the deeply connected sense that all are One.

Shimon bar Yohai (she-mone bahr yoe-khai): The mystic credited by tradition as an author of the Zohar, also known as Rashbi.

Shlah manot (shlah mah-not, shlah mah-nes): Purim practice of "sending" sweets as presents to friends, family, and the needy in celebration of the freedom gained in the Purim story.

shmurah matzah (sh'mooruh matzuh): Precisely prepared, handmade, circular matzah.

shmutz (shmuh-tz): Yiddish for getting dirty; can happen to face, clothes, hands, home, and soul.

shoah (shoh-ah); Destruction. Yom HaShoah is the term for Holocaust Memorial Day.

shofar (shoh-far): Ram's horn sounded each day of the lunar month of Elul leading up to Rosh HaShannah, on the

Jewish New Year itself and as Yom Kippur ends; symbol of the wake-up call to Abraham not to misunderstand the intent of G*d and thereby sacrifice his son; its contemporary function is to help us to find our own wake-up calls when the sound pierces through our unawareness. In ancient times, the shofar was sounded from mountaintops to alert the next town of the changing of the month and year.

shomer Shabbat (show-mehr shah-baht, show-merhr Shah-bus): A person who is observant of Shabbat practices such as not traveling, cooking, or turning on appliances.

shpiel (shpeel): Yiddish for a quick, story-style telling.

shrei gevalt (shrei g'vahlt): Yiddish for "cry out— enough!" *Gevalt* can also have a flip-side meaning of "it was more than enough," implying ecstasy.

Siman Tov (see-mahn tove): A good sign. Title of a joyous occasion life-cycle song asking for the alignment of the stars on the date of the occasion to be auspicious for good things for those for whom the celebration is being held.

simha (sihm-huh): Happiness, rejoicing. Term for a joyous celebration and occasion such as a wedding, bar/bat mitzvah, bris, or baby-naming.

Simhat Torah (sihm-haht toh-rah, sim-hus toh-ruh): Holy day of rejoicing in completion of the year's cycle of reading the Torah and starting anew.

sitra ahrah (sit-ruh ah-ruh): Literally, "the other side." Refers to the shadow side that recedes during Shabbat practice yet likely will recur under the stresses of the week.

siyyum (see-yoom): Practice of creating a gathering in which one offers a teaching that summarizes a recently completed cycle of study of a major work, such as of a volume of the Talmud or, more recently, of the Encyclopedia Judaica.

ska<u>h</u> (s'kah<u>h</u>): Branches one gathers to lay atop the roof slats of a *sukkah* to create a natural filtering of light, air, and rain.

sufganiot (soof-gah-nee-ote): Israeli-style donut delicacy served on <u>H</u>anukkah.

sukkah (soo-kah, also often pronounced suh-kah): Annual harvest hut built in one's yard for partaking meals and use of the symbols of the Sukkot festival, the *lulav* and *etrog*. Puts one in touch with the fragility and beauty of life in the context of nature, as the ceiling must let in sunlight, moonlight, and rain. Builds community through the mitzvah of inviting others to dine in your *sukkah*.

Sukkot (soo-coat, suh-kus): Name of harvest festival; see above.

taanit (tah-ah-neet, possessive form): Fast of. Another term for fast is *tzom*.

tashli<u>h</u> (tahsh-li<u>h</u>): Second day of Rosh HaShannah ritual for gathering awareness within yourself of aspects of the year or qualities within yourself that you hope to transform for the better. These hopes are symbolically placed into crumbs and *tashli<u>h</u>*, "sent" away in a body of water as energy for the fish to consume and put to better use.

tefillin (t'fee-leen, t'fih-lihn): Tool for focused morning meditation that involves specific prayers said while wrapping leather straps on the head and non-dominant arm. One leather box is attached to each strap containing verses from Torah that emphasize listening, loving, and leading a mitzvah-centered life.

teshuvah (t'shoo-vah): Efforts to repair negative energy in a relationship by "turning yourself." Efforts can be within yourself, another, the environment, and G*d.

tikkun (tee-koon, tih-kn): Repair or renewal of matters and nature on this planet.

tikkun leyl Shavuot (tee-koon leyl shah-voo-ote, tih-kn leyl Shavu-uhs): Practice of staying up all night in study before the dawning of Shavuot, the day of the festival commemorating the giving of the Torah at Sinai.

tzelem (tzeh-lehm): Image. Torah describes humans as *b'tzelem Elohim*, in the image of G*d.

tzimmis (tzih-muhs): Side dish of sweet potatoes and dried plums or prunes baked with honey served on holidays and Shabbat.

tzom (tzohm): Fast by neither eating nor drinking. Jewish fasting practice is not intended to afflict oneself; rather, the expectation is that one's mind is so focused on prayer and reflection on certain set holy days that one transcends the need for food.

Tzom Gedaliah (tzohm g'dahl-ee-ah): Fast commemorating the Babylonians' brutality toward Jews during their reign over those who remained living in Israel.

upsherin (oop-shehr'n:) Ritual of waiting until about age three for a child's first haircut, signifying the transition from toddler to child through their ability to learn, understand, and replicate behaviors. A first Hebrew letter is often taught at this time.

ushpizin (oosh-pea-zihn): Aramaic for guests; a *sukkah* ritual of inviting in spirits of important ancestors who were biblical and prophetic figures, as well as great leaders, sages, teachers, and family, the sense of whose presence will add to your *sukkah* experience.

viduii (vee-doo-ee): Confession of marks missed in life. Generally done on Yom Kippur in collective form (we have

polluted, for example) and at the end of life as a personal recollection of marks missed on the journey of life.

yahrzeit (yahr-tzeit): Literally, "one year of time" in
Yiddish. Signifies the anniversary of a person's death, which is
observed by loved ones by the lighting of a candle that will
burn for one day and by going to a prayer service where
Kaddish can be recited. It is also customary to know which
great sages and teachers died on any given day of the year and
to study the teachings of one of them as a path of personal
growth, to give honor to their memory, and to take in their
mazal, the shining qualities of a soul that transcend death.

yamim no'rah'im (yah-mim no'rah'im): Days of awe;
name given to the High Holy Days for their awesome and
fearsome quality of consciousness.

yehi ratzon (y'hee rah-tzohn): May it be desired; a quick
prayer for life to go as wished.

yetzirah (y'tzeer-ah): Kabbalists offer four dimensions of
spiritual practice; this one deals with the formation and
addressing of feelings.

yihud (yee-hud): Unification, experience of deep, complete unity; also term for private time for a couple immediately after their wedding ceremony.

yirah (year-ah): Awe and fear are the same word in
Hebrew. In Jewish literature we sometimes refer to ourselves
as *yirei haShem*, those in awe of G*d.

Yizkor (yihz-core): Special memorial service for deceased
loved ones.

yom (yome): Day. The Jewish model is for a day to go from
sundown to sundown; the day begins as evening commences.

Yom *HaDin* (yome hah-deen): Day of Judgment, one of the ways of referring to the aspect of raised awareness that expands with compassionate support and awe at the amazing evolving nature of creation that is highlighted on Rosh HaShannah.

Yom *Kippur Katan* (yome key-pour kah-tahn): Day before each New Moon, that is, a "little Yom Kippur" in the sense of engaging in self-reflection of marks missed in recent life and how best to redress those affected.

zikaron (zee-kah-rohn): Remembrance. Yom HaZikaron is one of the names in Torah for Rosh HaShannah and it is the official name for Israel's Memorial Day for veterans and MIAs.

z'man (z'mahn): Time, season. In prayers refers to a specific conjunction of planets that makes the season auspicious for the qualities being commemorated during the holy day; so Passover is a *z'man* that is auspicious for *heyruteynu,* "our freedom." Keep in mind that the Jewish calendar is lunar and that we have a long history of attention to astrological correspondences, as revealed in numerous Talmudic passages and archaeological findings in Israel.

Zohar (zoh-hahr): Foundational Jewish mystical text; written in Hebrew and Aramaic.

zoher Shabbat (zoe-hehr, shah-baht): One who remembers to support the spirit of a sweet and joyful Shabbat experience.

SUGGESTIONS FOR FURTHER READING

This bibliography is for those developing a holiday and Shabbat lifestyle with an emphasis upon meaning, relevance, and spirituality. An expanded version of this list with titles for life-cycle events, prayer, Torah study, mitzvot, Hebrew, peoplehood, and also works for more advanced students appears on the web at www.ReclaimingJudaism.org and is updated biannually. Please write with suggestions for additional works to post c/o rebgoldiem@aol.com.

Abramowitz, Yosef I., and Rabbi Susan Silverman. *Jewish Family and Life: Traditions, Holidays and Values for Today's Parents and Children*. New York: Golden Adult Books, 1997. Enthusiastic guide; sometimes spiritual, and truly useful for families.

Alter, Judah Aryeh Leib, Arthur Green (trans.), and Shai Gluskin. *The Language of Truth: The Torah Commentary of Sefat Emet*. Philadelphia: Jewish Publication Society, 1998. Makes accessible the inspiring words of a remarkable

Hasidic commentator cited in *Reclaiming Judaism*. His style is open to Jews from every part of Judaism.

Berrin, Susan, ed. *Celebrating the New Moon: A Rosh Chodesh Anthology*. Northvale, N.J.: Jason Aronson, 1996. Great guide for Jewish women's New Moon ritual/support gatherings.

Bonder, Nilton. *The Kabbalah of Envy: Transforming Hatred, Anger and Other Negative Emotions*. Boston: Shambhala, 1997. While not Kabbalah in the current sense, this book is part of a series that gives easy access to ethical guidance, very human.

Brener, Anne. *Mourning and Mitzvah: A Guided Journal for Walking the Mourner's Path Through Grief and Healing*. Woodstock, Vt.: Jewish Lights, 2001. Best book I have found for combining Jewish spirituality with our deep, traditional mourning practices and a creative therapeutic approach. Remains helpful as *yahrzeits* and *yizkor* approach.

Buxbaum, Yitzhak. *Jewish Spiritual Practices*. Northvale, N.J.: Jason Aronson, 1990. Amazing, fascinating source reader on Hasidic stories and passages which can inspire our own spiritual growth. Has specific sections for holidays and Shabbat.

Cooper, David A. *God Is a Verb: Kabbalah and the Practice of Mystical Judaism*. New York: Penguin, 1998. Beautiful and inspiring expression of Jewish practice for our times. Attend services after reading this with more ways to authentically connect to Judaism, liturgy, and G*d.

———. *The Handbook of Jewish Meditation Practices: A Guide for Enriching the Sabbath and Other Days of Your Life*. Woodstock, Vt.: Jewish Lights, 2000. Start your practice now; accessible, clear, inspiring.

Davis, Avram, ed. *Meditation from the Heart of Judaism: Today's Teachers Share Their Practices, Techniques and Faith*. Woodstock, Vt.: Jewish Lights, 1997. Excellent collection of essays by the first wave of Western Jewish meditation teachers.

Diament, Carol, ed. *Moonbeams: A Hadassah Rosh Hodesh Guide*. Woodstock, Vt.: Jewish Lights, 2000. Informative and clear guide for every Jewish girl or woman.

Dosick, Wayne. *Soul Judaism: Dancing with God into a New Era*. Woodstock, Vt.: Jewish Lights, 1999. Sweet overview of applied Jewish spirituality for holidays and daily living; strong Carlebach influence.

Elkins, Dov Peretz. *Jewish Guided Imagery: A How-To Book for Rabbis, Educators and Group Leaders*. Princeton, N.J.: Growth Associates, 1996. Easy, meaningful, and sometimes spiritual imagery to incorporate into holidays, services, and group events.

Elon, Ari, Naomi Mara Hyman, and Arthur Waskow, eds. *Trees, Earth and Torah: A Tu B'Shvat Anthology*. Philadelphia: Jewish Publication Society, 2003. Substantial compilation of translated traditional sources on Judaism and the environment.

Falcon, Ted. *A Journey of Awakening: Kabbalistic Meditations on the Tree of Life*, rev. ed. Seattle: Hara, 2003. Available through www.betalef.org. Psycho-spiritual guide for each day of the *Omer* process.

Firestone, Tirzah. *The Receiving: Reclaiming Jewish Women's Wisdom*. San Francisco: Harper San Francisco, 2002. Restores seven ancient, remarkable Jewish women from talmudic and medieval times to our view and helps us find connections to them. Perfect to read in your *sukkah* as part of *ushpizin* practice.

Frankiel, Tamar. *The Gift of Kabbalah: Discovering the Secrets of Heaven, Renewing Your Life on Earth*. Woodstock, Vt.: Jewish Lights, 2001. Introduction to practical Kabbalah, easy to read and implement. Can help enlighten one's *Omer* practice.

Frankiel, Tamar, and Judy Greenfeld. *Minding the Temple of the Soul: Balancing Body, Mind and Spirit through Traditional Jewish Prayer, Movement and Meditation*. Woodstock, Vt.: Jewish Lights, 1997. Delightful guide that combines yoga-type movement traditions with Jewish prayer. Will help you expand your practice—I used this to develop a unique and very appreciated *tashlih* service.

Gefen, Nan Fink. *Discovering Jewish Meditation: Instruction and Guidance for Learning an Ancient Spiritual Practice*. Woodstock, Vt.: Jewish Lights, 1999. User-friendly introduction.

Ginsberg, Elliot. *The Sabbath in the Classical Kabbalah*. Albany, N.Y.: SUNY Press, 1989. Academic study that was eye-opening and very influential upon Rabbi Milgram's understanding of the deep structure of Shabbat mysticism.

Goldstein, Elyse. *The Women's Torah Commentary: New Insights from Women Rabbis on the 54 Weekly Torah Portions*. Woodstock, Vt.: Jewish Lights, 2001. This is Torah-live, brand new with views never heard before, from many. Her other works are equally wonderful support for your Shabbat Torah studies.

Green, Arthur. *Ehyeh: A Kabbalah for Tomorrow*. Woodstock, Vt.: Jewish Lights, 2004. Kabbalah-based theology suggestive of how to harmonize modernity with a desire for an accessible G*d. You can face Yom Kippur differently after reading this work and the next. Author has works that open up the language of Jewish spiritual practice.

————. *Seek My Face: A Jewish Mystical Theology*. Woodstock, Vt.: Jewish Lights, 2003. Solid Jewish philosophy through a deep soul for the times in which we live.

Greenbaum, Avraham. *The Wings of the Sun: Traditional Jewish Healing in Theory and Practice*. Jerusalem: Breslov Research Institute, 1995. Fascinating collection of Jewish healing traditions, focusing on those of Reb Nachman of Breslov in particular. Nice to read during the month of Elul.

————. *Under the Table and How to Get Up: Jewish Pathways to Spiritual Growth*. Jerusalem: Breslov Research Institute, 1991. Opens with a magnificent healing story. If someone in your life is acting like a turkey, read this, then contemplate *teshuvah* practices that might be applicable.

Hammer, Jill. *Sisters at Sinai: New Tales of Biblical Women*. Philadelphia: Jewish Publication Society, 2001. Biblical women come even more to life for contemporary readers through this rabbi's scholarly and creative lens. Great for *ushpizin* study on sukkot and also to open up characters in the Torah portion on Shabbat.

Heschel, Abraham Joshua. *The Sabbath: Its Meaning for the Modern Man*. Boston: Shambhala, 2003. The ultimate beautiful explanation of Shabbat; an exquisite book, as are all of his writings. Essential, inspiring spiritual reading despite the patriarchal language.

Jacobson, Simon. *The Counting of the Omer*. New York: Meaningful Life Center, 1996. Order from wisdomreb@aol.com. My favorite *Omer* guidebook, spiritual and psychological in intent. All of his works are fascinating spiritual readings that often reflect the teachings of the Lubavitcher Rebbe, *z"l*, in a contemporary tone.

Kaplan, Aryeh. *Jewish Meditation: A Practical Guide*. New York: Schocken Books, 1985. Classic, exceptional; when you are ready to advance seek out his other works.

Kaplan, Mordecai M. *Judaism as a Civilization: Toward a Reconstruction of American Jewish Life*. Philadelphia: Jewish Publication Society, 1994. Deeply empowering explanation of how Judaism has always evolved and continues to do so. Forms the basis of the intellectual underpinnings of how it is possible to reclaim Judaism with creativity and integrity.

Kushner, Lawrence. *Eyes Remade for Wonder: A Lawrence Kushner Reader*. Woodstock, Vt.: Jewish Lights, 1998. Lawrence Kushner's many works have led the way for many contemporary teachers of Jewish spiritual practice and are filled with accessible translations and interpretations of mystical ideas and texts.

Labowitz, Shoni. *Miraculous Living: A Guided Journey in Kabbalah Through the Ten Gates of the Tree of Life*. New York: Simon and Schuster, 1996. Accessible, interesting reading: a woman, born Orthodox, studies Buddhism, becomes a Jewish renewal rabbi in Florida, and writes this synthesis work. This model can be worked into your daily Elul or *Omer* practice.

Lerner, Michael. *Jewish Renewal: A Path to Healing and Transformation*. San Francisco: Harper Perennial, 1994. Foundational work that has helped support the Jewish spiritual renaissance; focuses mainly on issues of social and personal change through a Jewish lens.

Matlins, Stuart M., ed. *The Jewish Lights Spirituality Handbook: A Guide to Understanding, Exploring and Living a Spiritual Life*. Woodstock, Vt.: Jewish Lights, 2003. A great overview for those starting on this path.

Milgrom, Jo. *Handmade Midrash: Workshops in Visual Theology.* Philadelphia: Jewish Publication Society, 1992. A must for teachers and great for parents and artists and all open to experiencing Torah through your art and heart.

Morinis, Alan. *Climbing Jacob's Ladder: One Man's Journey to Rediscover a Jewish Spiritual Tradition.* New York: Broadway Books, 2002. Male spiritual journey book that also transforms the strict traditions of mussar into loving ways to pay attention to personal qualities that need work. Helpful for Elul, Kiddush Levanah, or *Omer* practice.

Muller, Wayne. *Sabbath: Finding Rest, Renewal and Delight in Our Busy Lives.* New York: Bantam, 2000. Reveals the core of Sabbath as a time out for renewal; powerfully motivational writing; very real.

Olitzky, Kerry M., and Daniel Judson, eds. *The Rituals & Practices of a Jewish Life: A Handbook for Personal Spiritual Renewal.* Woodstock, Vt.: Jewish Lights, 2002. Pieces from many leading teachers on important aspects of Jewish practice.

Ouaknin, Marc-Alain. *Mysteries of the Kabbalah.* New York: Abbeville, 1999. Excellent, clear description of history, major aspects of Kabbalah, and beautiful expression of the heart of the matter. Will support your *Omer* practice and other applications of the *sephirot* in your daily meditative life.

Pearl, Judea, and Ruth Pearl, eds. *I Am Jewish: Personal Reflections Inspired by the Last Words of Daniel Pearl.* Woodstock, Vt.: Jewish Lights, 2004. How do some of the most interesting and inspiring Jews find meaning through being Jewish? This is a powerful collection for all of us to read and discuss at the holiday and Shabbat table.

Plaskow, Judith. *Standing Again at Sinai: Judaism from a Feminist Perspective*. San Francisco: Harper San Francisco, 1991. This book changed Judaism for many of us, revealing how we are all truly invited to hear and interpret Torah anew in every generation. Great to read annually in preparation for Shavuot.

Prager, Marcia. *The Path of Blessing: Experiencing the Energy and Abundance of the Divine*. Woodstock, Vt.: Jewish Lights, 2003. Skillfully offers deeper understanding of Jewish blessing practices; why isn't this taught in Hebrew school?

Raphael, Simcha Paull. *Jewish Views of the Afterlife*. Northvale, N.J.: Jason Aronson, 1996. Yes, we do have a history of reincarnation as a Jewish belief. Fascinating reading with solid research behind it. See if *yizkor* changes for you after reading this.

Ribner, Melinda. *Kaballah Month by Month: A Year of Spiritual Practice and Personal Transformation*. San Francisco: Jossey-Bass, 2002. Reveals many fascinating traditions of Judaism that have astrological roots and applications. Perfect companion for Rosh Ḥodesh.

_____. *The Gift of a New Beginning* (order by writing to the author at 332 W. 87th St., NY, NY 10024). Excellent guide to *teshuvah* as an inner and inter-human process.

Schachter-Shalomi, Zalman. *Gate to the Heart: An Evolving Process*. Available at www.aleph.org. Exquisite little book by the founder of the Jewish renewal phenomenon offers accessible, deep spiritual guidance on *teshuvah* and other core practices. His many works really define Jewish spiritual practice for our times.

Schachter-Shalomi, Zalman, and Donald Gropman. *First Steps to a New Jewish Spirit: Reb Zalman's Guide to*

Recapturing the Intimacy and Ecstasy in Your Relationship with God. Woodstock, Vt.: Jewish Lights, 2003. An early work reflecting ideas of Reb Zalman; this work has helped many reclaim Judaism.

Shapira, Kalonymus Kalman. *Conscious Community: A Guide to Inner Work.* Northvale, N.J.: Jason Aronson, 1996. Very interesting to read and then reflect on your own community and the *teshuvah* that becomes needed from unhealthy interactions. The author was called the Piacetzna rebbe. Co-interpreted by Rabbi Andrea Cohen-Kiener and Yosef Grodsky.

Shapiro, Rami. *Minyan: Ten Principles for Living a Life of Integrity.* New York: Bell Tower, 1997. Clear, simple, effective guide to Jewish spiritual practice with a Buddhist flavor.

_____. *This Is the Path: 12-Step Programs in a Jewish Context.* Available through simplyjewish.com, where his many fascinating self-published works can be accessed. Excellent and not just for substance abuse healing, this spirituality will also speak to those of us addicted to "time."

_____. *The Way of Solomon: Finding Joy and Contentment in the Wisdom of Ecclesiastes.* San Francisco: Harper San Francisco, 2000. Exquisite. Consider studying a section daily.

Siegel, Daniel, ed. *Siddur Kol Koreh.* Available through www.aleph.org. Spiritually uplifting translations of every prayer in the Shabbat service and many very moving contemporary liturgical additions (looseleaf binder format).

Steinsaltz, Adin. *The Strife of the Spirit.* Northvale, N.J.: Jason Aronson, 1988. Speaks like breath, right into one's soul; beautiful work for those doing *teshuvah* under difficult circumstances. Everything he has written proves valuable.

Strassfeld, Michael. *The Jewish Holidays: A Guide and Commentary*. New York: Harper, 1985. Very helpful and clear for grasping the basics of Jewish holiday practices.

Strassfeld, Michael, and Joy Levitt, eds. *A Night of Questions: A Passover Haggadah*. Philadelphia: The Reconstructionist Press, 2000. Brings the seder alive in a colorful, entry-level, user-friendly way, a major improvement on most haggadot; companion music tape also available via www.JRF.org.

Telushkin, Joseph. *Words That Hurt, Words That Heal*. New York: Quill Press, 1998. Eloquent and easy-to-grasp principles of the spirituality in how we speak to and treat others. Reread this every Elul and read it aloud to children and spouse to spark discussion and growth.

Waskow, Arthur. *Seasons of Our Joy: A Modern Guide to the Jewish Holidays*. Boston: Beacon, 1982. Valuable; the original spiritual guide for the holidays from a leader of the movement for Jewish renewal. Author has many valuable works, some self-published; visit www.shalomctr.org.

Weinberg, Matis. *Frameworks* series. Jerusalem: Foundation for Jewish Publication, 1998. Torah commentaries mining spiritual possibilities from traditional and mystical sources; deep, accessible. Expect to have to work past some patriarchal bias.

Wiener, Shohama. ed. *The Fifty-Eighth Century: A Jewish Renewal Sourcebook*. Northvale, N.J.: Jason Aronson, 1996. Lots of creative essays that open up the methods of joyful Jewishing for holidays and many other aspects of Jewish life.

Wiener, Shohama Harris, and Jonathan Omer-Man. *Worlds of Jewish Prayer: A Festschrift in Honor of Rabbi Zalman M. Schachter-Shalomi*. Northvale, N.J.: Jason Aronson, 1993. More of the above.

Wieseltier, Leo. *Kaddish*. New York: Knopf, 1998. Deep reading.

Winkler, Gershon. *The Way of the Boundary Crosser: An Introduction to Jewish Flexidoxy*. Northvale, N.J.: Jason Aronson, 1998. Very helpful understanding of how to deal with the apparent inflexibility of halahah when your spirituality and personal values seem in conflict with Judaism.

Winkler, Gershon, and Lakme Batya Elior. *The Place Where You Are Standing Is Holy: A Jewish Theology on Human Relationships*. Northvale, N.J.: Jason Aronson, 1998. From Orthodox background to highly creative contemporary new Jewish lifestyle, this unique clergy couple reflects on bringing holiness and *teshuvah* practice into your marriage in any part of the spectrum.

Yerushalmi, Yosef Hayim. *Zakhor: Jewish History and Jewish Memory*. Seattle: University of Washington Press, 1982. A gem, I read it when it came out and re-read it with benefit recently. Exquisite essays that touch the heart of memory and the memorial aspects of High Holy Day and Shabbat services and practices.

Zaslow, David. *Ivdu Et HaShem B'Simcha: A Siddur for Spiritual Renewal*. 1997. (Orders via the author, 692 Elkader St., Ashland, OR 97520. E-mail ShalomRav@aol.com.) Excellent soft-back Shabbat siddur with nice large typeface; richly spiritual orientation of translations and many joyful songs included.

Ziff, Joel. *Mirrors in Time: A Psycho-Spiritual Journey through the Jewish Year*. Northvale, N.J.: Jason Aronson, 1996. Important spiritual analysis of the holidays for clergy, therapists, and educators.

Zornberg, Avivah Gottlieb. *The Beginning of Desire: Reflections on Genesis*. New York: Image Books, 1996. Scholarship and spirit combine to yield a fascinating and highly informative tour into the biblical book of Genesis.

————. *The Particulars of Rapture: Reflections on Exodus*. New York: Image Books, 2002. More of the above, applied to Exodus.

INDEX

NOTES

NOTES

NOTES

NOTES

NOTES

Bar/Bat Mitzvah

The Bar/Bat Mitzvah Memory Book
An Album for Treasuring the Spiritual Celebration
By Rabbi Jeffrey K. Salkin and Nina Salkin
A unique album for preserving the spiritual memories of the day, and for recording plans for the Jewish future ahead. Contents include space for creating or recording family history; teachings received from rabbi, cantor, and others; mitzvot and *tzedakot* chosen and carried out, etc.
8 x 10, 48 pp, Deluxe Hardcover, 2-color text, ribbon marker, ISBN 1-58023-111-X **$19.95**

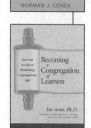

Bar/Bat Mitzvah Basics: A Practical Family Guide to Coming of Age Together
Edited by Helen Leneman. Foreword by Rabbi Jeffrey K. Salkin.
6 x 9, 240 pp, Quality PB, ISBN 1-58023-151-9 **$18.95**

For Kids—Putting God on Your Guest List: How to Claim the Spiritual Meaning of Your Bar or Bat Mitzvah *By Rabbi Jeffrey K. Salkin*
6 x 9, 144 pp, Quality PB, ISBN 1-58023-015-6 **$14.95** *For ages 11–12*

Putting God on the Guest List: How to Reclaim the Spiritual Meaning of Your Child's Bar or Bat Mitzvah *By Rabbi Jeffrey K. Salkin*
6 x 9, 224 pp, Quality PB, ISBN 1-879045-59-1 **$16.95**

Tough Questions Jews Ask: A Young Adult's Guide to Building a Jewish Life
By Rabbi Edward Feinstein 6 x 9, 160 pp, Quality PB, ISBN 1-58023-139-X **$14.95** *For ages 13 & up*
Also Available: **Tough Questions Jews Ask Teacher's Guide**
8½ x 11, 72 pp, PB, ISBN 1-58023-187-X **$8.95**

Bible Study/Midrash

Hineini in Our Lives: Learning How to Respond to Others through 14 Biblical Texts, and Personal Stories *By Norman J. Cohen*
6 x 9, 240 pp, Hardcover, ISBN 1-58023-131-4 **$23.95**

Ancient Secrets: Using the Stories of the Bible to Improve Our Everyday Lives
By Rabbi Levi Meier, Ph.D. 5½ x 8½, 288 pp, Quality PB, ISBN 1-58023-064-4 **$16.95**

Moses—The Prince, the Prophet: His Life, Legend & Message for Our Lives
By Rabbi Levi Meier, Ph.D.
6 x 9, 224 pp, Quality PB, ISBN 1-58023-069-5 **$16.95**

Self, Struggle & Change: Family Conflict Stories in Genesis and Their Healing Insights for Our Lives *By Norman J. Cohen* 6 x 9, 224 pp, Quality PB, ISBN 1-879045-66-4 **$16.95**

Voices from Genesis: Guiding Us through the Stages of Life *By Norman J. Cohen*
6 x 9, 192 pp, Quality PB, ISBN 1-58023-118-7 **$16.95**

Congregation Resources

Becoming a Congregation of Learners: Learning as a Key to Revitalizing Congregational Life *By Isa Aron, Ph.D. Foreword by Rabbi Lawrence A. Hoffman.*
6 x 9, 304 pp, Quality PB, ISBN 1-58023-089-X **$19.95**

Finding a Spiritual Home: How a New Generation of Jews Can Transform the American Synagogue *By Rabbi Sidney Schwarz*
6 x 9, 352 pp, Quality PB, ISBN 1-58023-185-3 **$19.95**

Jewish Pastoral Care: A Practical Handbook from Traditional & Contemporary Sources
Edited by Rabbi Dayle A. Friedman 6 x 9, 464 pp, Hardcover, ISBN 1-58023-078-4 **$35.00**

The Self-Renewing Congregation: Organizational Strategies for Revitalizing Congregational Life *By Isa Aron, Ph.D. Foreword by Dr. Ron Wolfson.*
6 x 9, 304 pp, Quality PB, ISBN 1-58023-166-7 **$19.95**

Or phone, fax, mail or e-mail to: **JEWISH LIGHTS** Publishing
Sunset Farm Offices, Route 4 • P.O. Box 237 • Woodstock, Vermont 05091
Tel: (802) 457-4000 • Fax: (802) 457-4004 • www.jewishlights.com
Credit card orders: (800) 962-4544 (8:30AM–5:30PM ET Monday–Friday)
Generous discounts on quantity orders. SATISFACTION GUARANTEED. Prices subject to change.

Children's Books

What You Will See Inside a Synagogue
By Rabbi Lawrence A. Hoffman and Dr. Ron Wolfson; Full-color photos by Bill Aron

A colorful, fun-to-read introduction that explains the ways and whys of Jewish worship and religious life. Full-page photos; concise but informative descriptions of the objects used, the clergy and laypeople who have specific roles, and much more.

8½ x 10½, 32 pp, Full-color photos, Hardcover, ISBN 1-59473-012-1 **$17.99** *(A SkyLight Paths book)*

Because Nothing Looks Like God
By Lawrence and Karen Kushner

What is God like? Introduces children to the possibilities of spiritual life. Real-life examples of happiness and sadness invite us to explore, together with our children, the questions we all have about God.

11 x 8½, 32 pp, Full-color illus., Hardcover, ISBN 1-58023-092-X **$16.95** *For ages 4 & up*

Also Available: **Because Nothing Looks Like God Teacher's Guide**
8½ x 11, 22 pp, PB, ISBN 1-58023-140-3 **$6.95** *For ages 5–8*

Board Book Companions to *Because Nothing Looks Like God*
5 x 5, 24 pp, Full-color illus., SkyLight Paths Board Books, **$7.95** each *For ages 0–4*

What Does God Look Like? ISBN 1-893361-23-3

How Does God Make Things Happen? ISBN 1-893361-24-1

Where Is God? ISBN 1-893361-17-9

The 11th Commandment: Wisdom from Our Children
by The Children of America

"If there were an Eleventh Commandment, what would it be?" Children of many religious denominations across America answer in their own drawings and words.

8 x 10, 48 pp, Full-color illus., Hardcover, ISBN 1-879045-46-X **$16.95** *For all ages*

Jerusalem of Gold: Jewish Stories of the Enchanted City
Retold by Howard Schwartz. Full-color illus. by Neil Waldman.

A beautiful and engaging collection of historical and legendary stories for children. Based on Talmud, midrash, Jewish folklore, and mystical and Hasidic sources.

8 x 10, 64 pp, Full-color illus., Hardcover, ISBN 1-58023-149-7 **$18.95** *For ages 7 & up*

The Book of Miracles: A Young Person's Guide to Jewish Spiritual Awareness
By Lawrence Kushner. All-new illustrations by the author.

6 x 9, 96 pp, 2-color illus., Hardcover, ISBN 1-879045-78-8 **$16.95** *For ages 9–13*

In Our Image: God's First Creatures
By Nancy Sohn Swartz

9 x 12, 32 pp, Full-color illus., Hardcover, ISBN 1-879045-99-0 **$16.95** *For ages 4 & up*

Also Available as a Board Book: **How Did the Animals Help God?**
5 x 5, 24 pp, Board, Full-color illus., ISBN 1-59473-044-X **$7.99** *For ages 0–4 (A SkyLight Paths book)*

From SKYLIGHT PATHS PUBLISHING

Becoming Me: A Story of Creation
By Martin Boroson. Full-color illus. by Christopher Gilvan-Cartwright.

Told in the personal "voice" of the Creator, a story about creation and relationship that is about each one of us.

8 x 10, 32 pp, Full-color illus., Hardcover, ISBN 1-893361-11-X **$16.95** *For ages 4 & up*

Ten Amazing People: And How They Changed the World
By Maura D. Shaw. Foreword by Dr. Robert Coles. Full-color illus. by Stephen Marchesi.

Black Elk • Dorothy Day • Malcolm X • Mahatma Gandhi • Martin Luther King, Jr. • Mother Teresa • Janusz Korczak • Desmond Tutu • Thich Nhat Hanh • Albert Schweitzer.

8½ x 11, 48 pp, Full-color illus., Hardcover, ISBN 1-893361-47-0 **$17.95** *For ages 7 & up*

Where Does God Live? *By August Gold and Matthew J. Perlman*

Helps young readers develop a personal understanding of God.

10 x 8½, 32 pp, Full-color photo illus., Quality PB, ISBN 1-893361-39-X **$8.99** *For ages 3–6*

Children's Books
by Sandy Eisenberg Sasso

Adam & Eve's First Sunset: God's New Day
Engaging new story explores fear and hope, faith and gratitude in ways that will delight kids and adults—inspiring us to bless each of God's days and nights.
9 x 12, 32 pp, Full-color illus., Hardcover, ISBN 1-58023-177-2 **$17.95** *For ages 4 & up*

But God Remembered
Stories of Women from Creation to the Promised Land
Four different stories of women—Lillith, Serach, Bityah, and the Daughters of Z—teach us important values through their faith and actions.
9 x 12, 32 pp, Full-color illus., Hardcover, ISBN 1-879045-43-5 **$16.95** *For ages 8 & up*

Cain & Abel: Finding the Fruits of Peace
Shows children that we have the power to deal with anger in positive ways. Provides questions for kids and adults to explore together.
9 x 12, 32 pp, Full-color illus., Hardcover, ISBN 1-58023-123-3 **$16.95** *For ages 5 & up*

God in Between
If you wanted to find God, where would you look? This magical, mythical tale teaches that God can be found where we are: within all of us and the relationships between us.
9 x 12, 32 pp, Full-color illus., Hardcover, ISBN 1-879045-86-9 **$16.95** *For ages 4 & up*

God's Paintbrush: Special 10th Anniversary Edition
Wonderfully interactive, invites children of all faiths and backgrounds to encounter God through moments in their own lives. Provides questions adult and child can explore together.
11 x 8½, 32 pp, Full-color illus., Hardcover, ISBN 1-58023-195-0 **$17.95** *For ages 4 & up*

Also Available: **God's Paintbrush Teacher's Guide**
8½ x 11, 32 pp, PB, ISBN 1-879045-57-5 **$8.95**

God's Paintbrush Celebration Kit
A Spiritual Activity Kit for Teachers and Students of All Faiths, All Backgrounds
Additional activity sheets available:
8-Student Activity Sheet Pack (40 sheets/5 sessions), ISBN 1-58023-058-X **$19.95**
Single-Student Activity Sheet Pack (5 sessions), ISBN 1-58023-059-8 **$3.95**

In God's Name
Like an ancient myth in its poetic text and vibrant illustrations, this award-winning modern fable about the search for God's name celebrates the diversity and, at the same time, the unity of all people.
9 x 12, 32 pp, Full-color illus., Hardcover, ISBN 1-879045-26-5 **$16.99** *For ages 4 & up*

Also Available as a Board Book: **What Is God's Name?**
5 x 5, 24 pp, Board, Full-color illus., ISBN 1-893361-10-1 **$7.99** *For ages 0–4* *(A SkyLight Paths book)*

Also Available: **In God's Name video and study guide**
Computer animation, original music, and children's voices. 18 min. **$29.99**

Also Available in Spanish: **El nombre de Dios**
9 x 12, 32 pp, Full-color illus., Hardcover, ISBN 1-893361-63-2 **$16.95** *(A SkyLight Paths book)*

Noah's Wife: The Story of Naamah
When God tells Noah to bring the animals of the world onto the ark, God also calls on Naamah, Noah's wife, to save each plant on Earth. Based on an ancient text.
9 x 12, 32 pp, Full-color illus., Hardcover, ISBN 1-58023-134-9 **$16.95** *For ages 4 & up*

Also Available as a Board Book: **Naamah, Noah's Wife**
5 x 5, 24 pp, Full-color illus., Board, ISBN 1-893361-56-X **$7.95** *For ages 0–4* *(A SkyLight Paths book)*

For Heaven's Sake: Finding God in Unexpected Places
9 x 12, 32 pp, Full-color illus., Hardcover, ISBN 1-58023-054-7 **$16.95** *For ages 4 & up*

God Said Amen: Finding the Answers to Our Prayers
9 x 12, 32 pp, Full-color illus., Hardcover, ISBN 1-58023-080-6 **$16.95** *For ages 4 & up*

Current Events/History

The Story of the Jews: A 4,000-Year Adventure—A Graphic History Book
Written & illustrated by Stan Mack
Through witty, illustrated narrative, we visit all the major happenings from biblical times to the twenty-first century. Celebrates the major characters and events that have shaped the Jewish people and culture.
6 x 9, 288 pp, illus., Quality PB, ISBN 1-58023-155-1 **$16.95**

The Jewish Prophet: Visionary Words from Moses and Miriam to Henrietta Szold and A. J. Heschel *By Rabbi Michael J. Shire*
6½ x 8½, 128 pp, 123 full-color illus., Hardcover, ISBN 1-58023-168-3 **$25.00**

Shared Dreams: Martin Luther King, Jr. & the Jewish Community
By Rabbi Marc Schneier. Preface by Martin Luther King III.
6 x 9, 240 pp, Hardcover, ISBN 1-58023-062-8 **$24.95**

"Who Is a Jew?": Conversations, Not Conclusions *By Meryl Hyman*
6 x 9, 272 pp, Quality PB, ISBN 1-58023-052-0 **$16.95**

Ecology

Ecology & the Jewish Spirit: Where Nature & the Sacred Meet
Edited by Ellen Bernstein 6 x 9, 288 pp, Quality PB, ISBN 1-58023-082-2 **$16.95**

Torah of the Earth: Exploring 4,000 Years of Ecology in Jewish Thought
Vol. 1: Biblical Israel: One Land, One People; Rabbinic Judaism: One People, Many Lands
Vol. 2: Zionism: One Land, Two Peoples; Eco-Judaism: One Earth, Many Peoples
Edited by Rabbi Arthur Waskow
Vol. 1: 6 x 9, 272 pp, Quality PB, ISBN 1-58023-086-5 **$19.95**
Vol. 2: 6 x 9, 336 pp, Quality PB, ISBN 1-58023-087-3 **$19.95**

Grief/Healing

Against the Dying of the Light: A Parent's Story of Love, Loss and Hope
By Leonard Fein
In this unusual exploration of heartbreak and healing, Leonard Fein chronicles the sudden death of his 30-year-old daughter and shares the hard-earned wisdom that emerges in the face of loss and grief.
5½ x 8½, 176 pp, Quality PB, ISBN 1-58023-197-7 **$15.99**

Grief in Our Seasons: A Mourner's Kaddish Companion *By Rabbi Kerry M. Olitzky*
4½ x 6½, 448 pp, Quality PB, ISBN 1-879045-55-9 **$15.95**

Healing of Soul, Healing of Body: Spiritual Leaders Unfold the Strength & Solace in Psalms *Edited by Rabbi Simkha Y. Weintraub, C.S.W.*
6 x 9, 128 pp, 2-color illus. text, Quality PB, ISBN 1-879045-31-1 **$14.95**

Jewish Paths toward Healing and Wholeness: A Personal Guide to Dealing with Suffering *By Rabbi Kerry M. Olitzky. Foreword by Debbie Friedman.*
6 x 9, 192 pp, Quality PB, ISBN 1-58023-068-7 **$15.95**

Mourning & Mitzvah, 2nd Edition: A Guided Journal for Walking the Mourner's Path through Grief to Healing *By Anne Brener, L.C.S.W.*
7½ x 9, 304 pp, Quality PB, ISBN 1-58023-113-6 **$19.95**

The Perfect Stranger's Guide to Funerals and Grieving Practices
A Guide to Etiquette in Other People's Religious Ceremonies *Edited by Stuart M. Matlins*
6 x 9, 240 pp, Quality PB, ISBN 1-893361-20-9 **$16.95** *(A SkyLight Paths book)*

Tears of Sorrow, Seeds of Hope: A Jewish Spiritual Companion for Infertility and Pregnancy Loss *By Rabbi Nina Beth Cardin*
6 x 9, 192 pp, Hardcover, ISBN 1-58023-017-2 **$19.95**

A Time to Mourn, A Time to Comfort: A Guide to Jewish Bereavement and Comfort *By Dr. Ron Wolfson* 7 x 9, 336 pp, Quality PB, ISBN 1-879045-96-6 **$18.95**

When a Grandparent Dies: A Kid's Own Remembering Workbook for Dealing with Shiva and the Year Beyond *By Nechama Liss-Levinson, Ph.D.*
8 x 10, 48 pp, 2-color text, Hardcover, ISBN 1-879045-44-3 **$15.95** *For ages 7–13*

Abraham Joshua Heschel

The Earth Is the Lord's: The Inner World of the Jew in Eastern Europe
5½ x 8, 128 pp, Quality PB, ISBN 1-879045-42-7 **$14.95**

Israel: An Echo of Eternity *New Introduction by Susannah Heschel*
5½ x 8, 272 pp, Quality PB, ISBN 1-879045-70-2 **$19.95**

A Passion for Truth: Despair and Hope in Hasidism
5½ x 8, 352 pp, Quality PB, ISBN 1-879045-41-9 **$18.99**

Holidays/Holy Days

Reclaiming Judaism as a Spiritual Practice: Holy Days and Shabbat
By Rabbi Goldie Milgram
Provides a framework for understanding the powerful and often unexplained intellectual, emotional, and spiritual tools that are essential for a lively, relevant, and fulfilling Jewish spiritual practice. 7 x 9, 272 pp, Quality PB, ISBN 1-58023-205-1 **$19.99**

7th Heaven: Celebrating Shabbat with Rebbe Nachman of Breslov
By Moshe Mykoff with the Breslov Research Institute
Based on the teachings of Rebbe Nachman of Breslov. Explores the art of consciously observing Shabbat and understanding in-depth many of the day's traditional spiritual practices. 5⅛ x 8¼, 224 pp, Deluxe PB w/flaps, ISBN 1-58023-175-6 **$18.95**

The Women's Passover Companion
Women's Reflections on the Festival of Freedom
Edited by Rabbi Sharon Cohen Anisfeld, Tara Mohr, and Catherine Spector
Groundbreaking. A provocative conversation about women's relationships to Passover as well as the roots and meanings of women's seders.
6 x 9, 352 pp, Hardcover, ISBN 1-58023-128-4 **$24.95**

The Women's Seder Sourcebook
Rituals & Readings for Use at the Passover Seder
Edited by Rabbi Sharon Cohen Anisfeld, Tara Mohr, and Catherine Spector
Gathers the voices of more than one hundred women in readings, personal and creative reflections, commentaries, blessings, and ritual suggestions that can be incorporated into your Passover celebration as supplements to or substitutes for traditional passages of the haggadah.
6 x 9, 384 pp, Hardcover, ISBN 1-58023-136-5 **$24.95**

Creating Lively Passover Seders: A Sourcebook of Engaging Tales, Texts & Activities
By David Arnow, Ph.D. 7 x 9, 416 pp, Quality PB, ISBN 1-58023-184-5 **$24.99**

Hanukkah, 2nd Edition: The Family Guide to Spiritual Celebration
By Dr. Ron Wolfson. Edited by Joel Lurie Grishaver.
7 x 9, 240 pp, illus., Quality PB, ISBN 1-58023-122-5 **$18.95**

The Jewish Family Fun Book: Holiday Projects, Everyday Activities, and Travel Ideas with Jewish Themes *By Danielle Dardashti and Roni Sarig. Illus. by Avi Katz.*
6 x 9, 288 pp, 70+ b/w illus. & diagrams, Quality PB, ISBN 1-58023-171-3 **$18.95**

The Jewish Gardening Cookbook: Growing Plants & Cooking for
Holidays & Festivals *By Michael Brown* 6 x 9, 224 pp, 30+ illus., Quality PB, ISBN 1-58023-116-0 **$16.95**

The Jewish Lights Book of Fun Classroom Activities: Simple and Seasonal Projects for Teachers and Students *By Danielle Dardashti and Roni Sarig*
6 x 9, 240 pp, Quality PB, ISBN 1-58023-206-X **$19.99**

Passover, 2nd Edition: The Family Guide to Spiritual Celebration
By Dr. Ron Wolfson with Joel Lurie Grishaver 7 x 9, 352 pp, Quality PB, ISBN 1-58023-174-8 **$19.95**

Shabbat, 2nd Edition: The Family Guide to Preparing for and Celebrating the Sabbath
By Dr. Ron Wolfson 7 x 9, 320 pp, illus., Quality PB, ISBN 1-58023-164-0 **$19.95**

Sharing Blessings: Children's Stories for Exploring the Spirit of the Jewish Holidays
By Rahel Musleah and Michael Klayman
8½ x 11, 64 pp, Full-color illus., Hardcover, ISBN 1-879045-71-0 **$18.95** *For ages 6 & up*

Inspiration

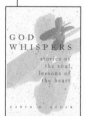

God in All Moments
Mystical & Practical Spiritual Wisdom from Hasidic Masters
Edited and translated by Or N. Rose with Ebn D. Leader
Hasidic teachings on how to be mindful in religious practice and cultivating everyday ethical behavior—*hanhagot*. 5½ x 8½, 192 pp, Quality PB, ISBN 1-58023-186-1 **$16.95**

Our Dance with God: Finding Prayer, Perspective and Meaning in the
Stories of Our Lives *By Karyn D. Kedar*
Inspiring spiritual insight to guide you on your life journeys and teach you to live and thrive in two conflicting worlds: the rational/material and the spiritual.
6 x 9, 176 pp, Quality PB, ISBN 1-58023-202-7 **$16.99**

Also Available: **The Dance of the Dolphin** (Hardcover edition of *Our Dance with God*)
6 x 9, 176 pp, Hardcover, ISBN 1-58023-154-3 **$19.95**

The Empty Chair: Finding Hope and Joy—Timeless Wisdom from a Hasidic Master,
Rebbe Nachman of Breslov *Adapted by Moshe Mykoff and the Breslov Research Institute*
4 x 6, 128 pp, 2-color text, Deluxe PB w/flaps, ISBN 1-879045-67-2 **$9.95**

The Gentle Weapon: Prayers for Everyday and Not-So-Everyday Moments—
Timeless Wisdom from the Teachings of the Hasidic Master, Rebbe Nachman of Breslov
Adapted by Moshe Mykoff and S. C. Mizrahi, together with the Breslov Research Institute
4 x 6, 144 pp, 2-color text, Deluxe PB w/flaps, ISBN 1-58023-022-9 **$9.95**

God Whispers: Stories of the Soul, Lessons of the Heart *By Karyn D. Kedar*
6 x 9, 176 pp, Quality PB, ISBN 1-58023-088-1 **$15.95**

An Orphan in History: One Man's Triumphant Search for His Jewish Roots
By Paul Cowan. Afterword by Rachel Cowan. 6 x 9, 288 pp, Quality PB, ISBN 1-58023-135-7 **$16.95**

Restful Reflections: Nighttime Inspiration to Calm the Soul, Based on Jewish Wisdom
By Rabbi Kerry M. Olitzky & Rabbi Lori Forman 4½ x 6½, 448 pp, Quality PB, ISBN 1-58023-091-1 **$15.95**

Sacred Intentions: Daily Inspiration to Strengthen the Spirit, Based on Jewish Wisdom
By Rabbi Kerry M. Olitzky and Rabbi Lori Forman 4½ x 6½, 448 pp, Quality PB, ISBN 1-58023-061-X **$15.95**

Kabbalah/Mysticism/Enneagram

Seek My Face: A Jewish Mystical Theology
By Dr. Arthur Green
This classic work of contemporary Jewish theology, revised and updated, is a profound, deeply personal statement of the lasting truths of Jewish mysticism and the basic faith claims of Judaism. A tool for anyone seeking the elusive presence of God in the world. 6 x 9, 304 pp, Quality PB, ISBN 1-58023-130-6 **$19.95**

Zohar: Annotated & Explained
Translation and annotation by Dr. Daniel C. Matt. Foreword by Andrew Harvey
Offers insightful yet unobtrusive commentary to the masterpiece of Jewish mysticism that explains references and mystical symbols, shares wisdom of spiritual masters, and clarifies the *Zohar*'s bold claim: We have always been taught that we need God, but in order to manifest in the world, God needs us.
5½ x 8½, 160 pp, Quality PB, ISBN 1-893361-51-9 **$15.99** *(A SkyLight Paths book)*

Cast in God's Image: Discover Your Personality Type Using the Enneagram and Kabbalah
By Rabbi Howard A. Addison
7 x 9, 176 pp, Quality PB, Layflat binding, 20+ journaling exercises, ISBN 1-58023-124-1 **$16.95**

Ehyeh: A Kabbalah for Tomorrow *By Dr. Arthur Green*
6 x 9, 224 pp, Quality PB, ISBN 1-58023-213-2 **$16.99**; Hardcover, ISBN 1-58023-125-X **$21.99**

The Enneagram and Kabbalah: Reading Your Soul *By Rabbi Howard A. Addison*
6 x 9, 176 pp, Quality PB, ISBN 1-58023-001-6 **$15.95**

Finding Joy: A Practical Spiritual Guide to Happiness *By Dannel I. Schwartz with Mark Hass*
6 x 9, 192 pp, Quality PB, ISBN 1-58023-009-1 **$14.95**; Hardcover, ISBN 1-879045-53-2 **$19.95**

The Gift of Kabbalah: Discovering the Secrets of Heaven, Renewing Your Life on Earth
By Tamar Frankiel, Ph.D.
6 x 9, 256 pp, Quality PB, ISBN 1-58023-141-1 **$16.95**; Hardcover, ISBN 1-58023-108-X **$21.95**

The Way Into Jewish Mystical Tradition *By Lawrence Kushner*
6 x 9, 224 pp, Quality PB, ISBN 1-58023-200-0 **$18.99**; Hardcover, ISBN 1-58023-029-6 **$21.95**

Life Cycle

Marriage / Parenting / Family / Aging

Jewish Fathers: A Legacy of Love
Photographs by Lloyd Wolf. Essays by Paula Wolfson. Foreword by Harold S. Kushner.
Honors the role of contemporary Jewish fathers in America. Each father tells in his own words what it means to be a parent and Jewish, and what he learned from his own father. Insightful photos. 9½ x 9⅞, 144 pp with 100+ duotone photos, Hardcover, ISBN 1-58023-204-3 **$30.00**

The New Jewish Baby Album: Creating and Celebrating the Beginning of a Spiritual Life—A Jewish Lights Companion
By the Editors at Jewish Lights. Foreword by Anita Diamant. Preface by Sandy Eisenberg Sasso.
A spiritual keepsake that will be treasured for generations. More than just a memory book, *shows you how—and why it's important*—to create a Jewish home and a Jewish life. 8 x 10, 64 pp, Deluxe Padded Hardcover, Full-color illus., ISBN 1-58023-138-1 **$19.95**

The Jewish Pregnancy Book: A Resource for the Soul, Body & Mind during Pregnancy, Birth & the First Three Months
By Sandy Falk, M.D., and Rabbi Daniel Judson, with Steven A. Rapp
Includes medical information on fetal development, pre-natal testing and more, from a liberal Jewish perspective; prenatal *Aleph-Bet* yoga; and prayers and rituals for each stage of pregnancy. 7 x 10, 208 pp, Quality PB, b/w illus., ISBN 1-58023-178-0 **$16.95**

Celebrating Your New Jewish Daughter: Creating Jewish Ways to Welcome Baby Girls into the Covenant—New and Traditional Ceremonies
By Debra Nussbaum Cohen 6 x 9, 272 pp, Quality PB, ISBN 1-58023-090-3 **$18.95**

The New Jewish Baby Book: Names, Ceremonies & Customs—A Guide for Today's Families *By Anita Diamant* 6 x 9, 336 pp, Quality PB, ISBN 1-879045-28-1 **$18.95**

Parenting As a Spiritual Journey: Deepening Ordinary and Extraordinary Events into Sacred Occasions *By Rabbi Nancy Fuchs-Kreimer* 6 x 9, 224 pp, Quality PB, ISBN 1-58023-016-4 **$16.95**

Embracing the Covenant: Converts to Judaism Talk About Why & How
Edited and with introductions by Rabbi Allan Berkowitz and Patti Moskovitz
6 x 9, 192 pp, Quality PB, ISBN 1-879045-50-8 **$16.95**

The Guide to Jewish Interfaith Family Life: An InterfaithFamily.com Handbook
Edited by Ronnie Friedland and Edmund Case 6 x 9, 384 pp, Quality PB, ISBN 1-58023-153-5 **$18.95**

Introducing My Faith and My Community
The Jewish Outreach Institute Guide for the Christian in a Jewish Interfaith Relationship *By Rabbi Kerry M. Olitzk.* 6 x 9, 176 pp, Quality PB, ISBN 1-58023-192-6 **$16.99**

Making a Successful Jewish Interfaith Marriage: The Jewish Outreach Institute Guide to Opportunities, Challenges and Resources
By Rabbi Kerry M. Olitzky with Joan Peterson Littman 6 x 9, 176 pp, Quality PB, ISBN 1-58023-170-5 **$16.95**

How to Be a Perfect Stranger, 3rd Edition: The Essential Religious Etiquette Handbook *Edited by Stuart M. Matlins and Arthur J. Magida*
The indispensable guide to the rituals and celebrations of the major religions and denominations in North America from the perspective of an interested guest of any other faith. 6 x 9, 432 pp, Quality PB, ISBN 1-893361-67-5 **$19.95** *(A SkyLight Paths book)*

The Creative Jewish Wedding Book: A Hands-On Guide to New & Old Traditions, Ceremonies & Celebrations *By Gabrielle Kaplan-Mayer*
Provides the tools to create the most meaningful Jewish traditional or alternative wedding by using ritual elements to express your unique style and spirituality.
9 x 9, 288 pp, b/w photos, Quality PB, ISBN 1-58023-194-2 **$19.99**

Divorce Is a Mitzvah: A Practical Guide to Finding Wholeness and Holiness When Your Marriage Dies *By Rabbi Perry Netter. Afterword by Rabbi Laura Geller.*
6 x 9, 224 pp, Quality PB, ISBN 1-58023-172-1 **$16.95**

A Heart of Wisdom: Making the Jewish Journey from Midlife through the Elder Years
Edited by Susan Berrin. Foreword by Harold Kushner. 6 x 9, 384 pp, Quality PB, ISBN 1-58023-051-2 **$18.95**

So That Your Values Live On: Ethical Wills and How to Prepare Them
Edited by Jack Riemer and Nathaniel Stampfer 6 x 9, 272 pp, Quality PB, ISBN 1-879045-34-6 **$18.95**

Meditation

The Handbook of Jewish Meditation Practices
A Guide for Enriching the Sabbath and Other Days of Your Life
By Rabbi David A. Cooper
Easy-to-learn meditation techniques for use on the Sabbath and every day, to help us return to the roots of traditional Jewish spirituality where Shabbat is a state of mind and soul. 6 x 9, 208 pp, Quality PB, ISBN 1-58023-102-0 **$16.95**

Discovering Jewish Meditation: Instruction & Guidance for Learning an Ancient Spiritual Practice *By Nan Fink Gefen, Ph.D.* 6 x 9, 208 pp, Quality PB, ISBN 1-58023-067-9 **$16.95**

A Heart of Stillness: A Complete Guide to Learning the Art of Meditation
By Rabbi David A. Cooper 5½ x 8½, 272 pp, Quality PB, ISBN 1-893361-03-9 **$16.95**
(A SkyLight Paths book)

Meditation from the Heart of Judaism: Today's Teachers Share Their Practices, Techniques, and Faith *Edited by Avram Davis*
6 x 9, 256 pp, Quality PB, ISBN 1-58023-049-0 **$16.95**

Silence, Simplicity & Solitude: A Complete Guide to Spiritual Retreat at Home
By Rabbi David A. Cooper 5½ x 8½, 336 pp, Quality PB, ISBN 1-893361-04-7 **$16.95**
(A SkyLight Paths book)

Three Gates to Meditation Practice: A Personal Journey into Sufism, Buddhism, and Judaism *By Rabbi David A. Cooper*
5½ x 8½, 240 pp, Quality PB, ISBN 1-893361-22-5 **$16.95** *(A SkyLight Paths book)*

The Way of Flame: A Guide to the Forgotten Mystical Tradition of Jewish Meditation
By Avram Davis 4½ x 8, 176 pp, Quality PB, ISBN 1-58023-060-1 **$15.95**

Ritual/Sacred Practice/Journaling

The Jewish Dream Book: The Key to Opening the Inner Meaning of Your Dreams *By Vanessa L. Ochs with Elizabeth Ochs; Full-color illus. by Kristina Swarner*
Instructions for how modern people can perform ancient Jewish dream practices and dream interpretations drawn from the Jewish wisdom tradition. For anyone who wants to understand their dreams—and themselves.
8 x 8, 120 pp, Full-color illus., Deluxe PB w/flaps, ISBN 1-58023-132-2 **$16.95**

The Jewish Journaling Book: How to Use Jewish Tradition to Write Your Life & Explore Your Soul *By Janet Ruth Falon*
Details the history of Jewish journaling throughout biblical and modern times, and teaches specific journaling techniques to help you create and maintain a vital journal, from a Jewish perspective. 8 x 8, 304 pp, Deluxe PB w/flaps, ISBN 1-58023-203-5 **$18.99**

The Rituals & Practices of a Jewish Life: A Handbook for Personal Spiritual Renewal *Edited by Rabbi Kerry M. Olitzky and Rabbi Daniel Judson*
6 x 9, 272 pp, illus., Quality PB, ISBN 1-58023-169-1 **$18.95**

The Book of Jewish Sacred Practices: CLAL's Guide to Everyday & Holiday Rituals & Blessings *Edited by Rabbi Irwin Kula and Vanessa L. Ochs, Ph.D.*
6 x 9, 368 pp, Quality PB, ISBN 1-58023-152-7 **$18.95**

Science Fiction/
Mystery & Detective Fiction

Mystery Midrash: An Anthology of Jewish Mystery & Detective Fiction
Edited by Lawrence W. Raphael. Preface by Joel Siegel.
6 x 9, 304 pp, Quality PB, ISBN 1-58023-055-5 **$16.95**

Criminal Kabbalah: An Intriguing Anthology of Jewish Mystery & Detective Fiction
Edited by Lawrence W. Raphael. Foreword by Laurie R. King.
6 x 9, 256 pp, Quality PB, ISBN 1-58023-109-8 **$16.95**

More Wandering Stars: An Anthology of Outstanding Stories of Jewish Fantasy and Science Fiction *Edited by Jack Dann. Introduction by Isaac Asimov.*
6 x 9, 192 pp, Quality PB, ISBN 1-58023-063-6 **$16.95**

Wandering Stars: An Anthology of Jewish Fantasy & Science Fiction
Edited by Jack Dann. Introduction by Isaac Asimov.
6 x 9, 272 pp, Quality PB, ISBN 1-58023-005-9 **$16.95**

Spirituality

The Alphabet of Paradise: An A–Z of Spirituality for Everyday Life
By Rabbi Howard Cooper
In twenty-six engaging chapters, Cooper spiritually illuminates the subjects of our daily lives—A to Z—examining these sources by using an ancient Jewish mystical method of interpretation that reveals both the literal and more allusive meanings of each.   5 x 7¼, 224 pp, Quality PB, ISBN 1-893361-80-2 **$16.95** *(A SkyLight Paths book)*

Does the Soul Survive?: A Jewish Journey to Belief in Afterlife, Past Lives & Living with Purpose   *By Rabbi Elie Kaplan Spitz. Foreword by Brian L Weiss, M.D.*
Spitz relates his own experiences and those shared with him by people he has worked with as a rabbi, and shows us that belief in afterlife and past lives, so often approached with reluctance, is in fact true to Jewish tradition.
6 x 9, 288 pp, Quality PB, ISBN 1-58023-165-9 **$16.95**; Hardcover, ISBN 1-58023-094-6 **$21.95**

First Steps to a New Jewish Spirit: Reb Zalman's Guide to Recapturing the Intimacy & Ecstasy in Your Relationship with God
By Rabbi Zalman M. Schachter-Shalomi with Donald Gropman
An extraordinary spiritual handbook that restores psychic and physical vigor by introducing us to new models and alternative ways of practicing Judaism. Offers meditation and contemplation exercises for enriching the most important aspects of everyday life.   6 x 9, 144 pp, Quality PB, ISBN 1-58023-182-9 **$16.95**

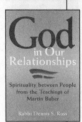

God in Our Relationships: Spirituality between People from the Teachings of Martin Buber   *By Rabbi Dennis S. Ross*
On the eightieth anniversary of Buber's classic work, we can discover new answers to critical issues in our lives. Inspiring examples from Ross's own life— as congregational rabbi, father, hospital chaplain, social worker, and husband— illustrate Buber's difficult-to-understand ideas about how we encounter God and each other. 5½ x 8½, 160 pp, Quality PB, ISBN 1-58023-147-0 **$16.95**

The Jewish Lights Spirituality Handbook: A Guide to Understanding, Exploring & Living a Spiritual Life   *Edited by Stuart M. Matlins*
What exactly is "Jewish" about spirituality? How do I make it a part of my life? Fifty of today's foremost spiritual leaders share their ideas and experience with us.
6 x 9, 456 pp, Quality PB, ISBN 1-58023-093-8 **$19.99**; Hardcover, ISBN 1-58023-100-4 **$24.95**

Bringing the Psalms to Life: How to Understand and Use the Book of Psalms
By Dr. Daniel F. Polish
6 x 9, 208 pp, Quality PB, ISBN 1-58023-157-8 **$16.95**; Hardcover, ISBN 1-58023-077-6 **$21.95**

God & the Big Bang: Discovering Harmony between Science & Spirituality
By Dr. Daniel C. Matt 6 x 9, 216 pp, Quality PB, ISBN 1-879045-89-3 **$16.95**

Godwrestling—Round 2: Ancient Wisdom, Future Paths
By Rabbi Arthur Waskow 6 x 9, 352 pp, Quality PB, ISBN 1-879045-72-9 **$18.95**

One God Clapping: The Spiritual Path of a Zen Rabbi   *By Rabbi Alan Lew with Sherril Jaffe*
5½ x 8½, 336 pp, Quality PB, ISBN 1-58023-115-2 **$16.95**

The Path of Blessing: Experiencing the Energy and Abundance of the Divine
By Rabbi Marcia Prager 5½ x 8½, 240 pp, Quality PB, ISBN 1-58023-148-9 **$16.95**

Six Jewish Spiritual Paths: A Rationalist Looks at Spirituality   *By Rabbi Rifat Sonsino*
6 x 9, 208 pp, Quality PB, ISBN 1-58023-167-5 **$16.95**; Hardcover, ISBN 1-58023-095-4 **$21.95**

Soul Judaism: Dancing with God into a New Era
By Rabbi Wayne Dosick 5½ x 8½, 304 pp, Quality PB, ISBN 1-58023-053-9 **$16.95**

Stepping Stones to Jewish Spiritual Living: Walking the Path Morning, Noon, and Night *By Rabbi James L. Mirel and Karen Bonnell Werth*
6 x 9, 240 pp, Quality PB, ISBN 1-58023-074-1 **$16.95**; Hardcover, ISBN 1-58023-003-2 **$21.95**

There Is No Messiah... and You're It: The Stunning Transformation of Judaism's Most Provocative Idea *By Rabbi Robert N. Levine, D.D.*
6 x 9, 192 pp, Hardcover, ISBN 1-58023-173-X **$21.95**

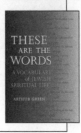

These Are the Words: A Vocabulary of Jewish Spiritual Life   *By Dr. Arthur Green*
6 x 9, 304 pp, Quality PB, ISBN 1-58023-107-1 **$18.95**

Spirituality/Lawrence Kushner

The Book of Letters: A Mystical Hebrew Alphabet
Popular Hardcover Edition, 6 x 9, 80 pp, 2-color text, ISBN 1-879045-00-1 **$24.95**
Deluxe Gift Edition with slipcase, 9 x 12, 80 pp, 4-color text, Hardcover, ISBN 1-879045-01-X **$79.95**
Collector's Limited Edition, 9 x 12, 80 pp, gold foil embossed pages, w/limited edition silkscreened print, ISBN 1-879045-04-4 **$349.00**

The Book of Miracles: A Young Person's Guide to Jewish Spiritual Awareness
All-new illustrations by the author
6 x 9, 96 pp, 2-color illus., Hardcover, ISBN 1-879045-78-8 **$16.95** *For ages 9–13*

The Book of Words: Talking Spiritual Life, Living Spiritual Talk
6 x 9, 160 pp, Quality PB, ISBN 1-58023-020-2 **$16.95**

Eyes Remade for Wonder: A Lawrence Kushner Reader
Introduction by Thomas Moore
6 x 9, 240 pp, Quality PB, ISBN 1-58023-042-3 **$18.95;** Hardcover, ISBN 1-58023-014-8 **$23.95**

God Was in This Place & I, i Did Not Know
Finding Self, Spirituality and Ultimate Meaning
6 x 9, 192 pp, Quality PB, ISBN 1-879045-33-8 **$16.95**

Honey from the Rock: An Introduction to Jewish Mysticism
6 x 9, 176 pp, Quality PB, ISBN 1-58023-073-3 **$16.95**

Invisible Lines of Connection: Sacred Stories of the Ordinary
5½ x 8½, 160 pp, Quality PB, ISBN 1-879045-98-2 **$15.95**

Jewish Spirituality—A Brief Introduction for Christians
5½ x 8½, 112 pp, Quality PB Original, ISBN 1-58023-150-0 **$12.95**

The River of Light: Jewish Mystical Awareness
6 x 9, 192 pp, Quality PB, ISBN 1-58023-096-2 **$16.95**

The Way Into Jewish Mystical Tradition
6 x 9, 224 pp, Quality PB, ISBN 1-58023-200-0 **$18.99;** Hardcover, ISBN 1-58023-029-6 **$21.95**

Spirituality/Prayer

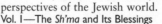

Pray Tell: A Hadassah Guide to Jewish Prayer
By Rabbi Jules Harlow, with contributions from Tamara Cohen, Rochelle Furstenberg, Rabbi Daniel Gordis, Leora Tanenbaum, and many others
A guide to traditional Jewish prayer enriched with insight and wisdom from a broad variety of viewpoints—from Orthodox, Conservative, Reform, and Reconstructionist Judaism to New Age and feminist.
8½ x 11, 400 pp, Quality PB, ISBN 1-58023-163-2 **$29.95**

My People's Prayer Book Series
Traditional Prayers, Modern Commentaries
Edited by Rabbi Lawrence A. Hoffman
Provides diverse and exciting commentary to the traditional liturgy, helping modern men and women find new wisdom in Jewish prayer, and bring liturgy into their lives. Each book includes Hebrew text, modern translation, and commentaries from all perspectives of the Jewish world.

Vol. 1—The *Sh'ma* and Its Blessings
7 x 10, 168 pp, Hardcover, ISBN 1-879045-79-6 **$23.95**
Vol. 2—The *Amidah*
7 x 10, 240 pp, Hardcover, ISBN 1-879045-80-X **$24.95**
Vol. 3—*P'sukei D'zimrah* (Morning Psalms)
7 x 10, 240 pp, Hardcover, ISBN 1-879045-81-8 **$24.95**
Vol. 4—*Seder K'riat Hatorah* (The Torah Service)
7 x 10, 264 pp, Hardcover, ISBN 1-879045-82-6 **$23.95**
Vol. 5—*Birkhot Hashachar* (Morning Blessings)
7 x 10, 240 pp, Hardcover, ISBN 1-879045-83-4 **$24.95**
Vol. 6—*Tachanun* and Concluding Prayers
7 x 10, 240 pp, Hardcover, ISBN 1-879045-84-2 **$24.95**
Vol. 7—Shabbat at Home
7 x 10, 240 pp, Hardcover, ISBN 1-879045-85-0 **$24.95**
Vol. 8—Shabbat in the Synagogue
7 x 10, 240 pp (est), Hardcover, ISBN 1-58023-121-7 **$24.99**

Spirituality/The Way Into... Series

The Way Into... Series offers an accessible and highly usable "guided tour" of the Jewish faith, people, history and beliefs—in total, an introduction to Judaism that will enable you to understand and interact with the sacred texts of the Jewish tradition. Each volume is written by a leading contemporary scholar and teacher, and explores one key aspect of Judaism. *The Way Into...* enables all readers to achieve a real sense of Jewish cultural literacy through guided study.

The Way Into Encountering God in Judaism *By Neil Gillman*
6 x 9, 240 pp, Quality PB, ISBN 1-58023-199-3 **$18.99**; Hardcover, ISBN 1-58023-025-3 **$21.95**

Also Available: **The Jewish Approach to God: A Brief Introduction for Christians**
By Neil Gillman 5½ x 8½, 192 pp, Quality PB, ISBN 1-58023-190-X **$16.95**

The Way Into Jewish Mystical Tradition *By Lawrence Kushner*
6 x 9, 224 pp, Quality PB, ISBN 1-58023-200-0 **$18.99**; Hardcover, ISBN 1-58023-029-6 **$21.95**

The Way Into Jewish Prayer *By Lawrence A. Hoffman*
6 x 9, 224 pp, Quality PB, ISBN 1-58023-201-9 **$18.99**; Hardcover, ISBN 1-58023-027-X **$21.95**

The Way Into Torah *By Norman J. Cohen*
6 x 9, 176 pp, Quality PB, ISBN 1-58023-198-5 **$16.99**; Hardcover, ISBN 1-58023-028-8 **$21.95**

Spirituality in the Workplace

Being God's Partner
How to Find the Hidden Link Between Spirituality and Your Work
By Rabbi Jeffrey K. Salkin. Introduction by Norman Lear.
6 x 9, 192 pp, Quality PB, ISBN 1-879045-65-6 **$17.95**

The Business Bible: 10 New Commandments for Bringing Spirituality & Ethical Values into the Workplace *By Rabbi Wayne Dosick*
5½ x 8½, 208 pp, Quality PB, ISBN 1-58023-101-2 **$14.95**

Spirituality and Wellness

Aleph-Bet Yoga
Embodying the Hebrew Letters for Physical and Spiritual Well-Being
By Steven A. Rapp. Foreword by Tamar Frankiel, Ph.D., and Judy Greenfeld. Preface by Hart Lazer
7 x 10, 128 pp, b/w photos, Quality PB, Layflat binding, ISBN 1-58023-162-4 **$16.95**

Entering the Temple of Dreams
Jewish Prayers, Movements, and Meditations for the End of the Day
By Tamar Frankiel, Ph.D., and Judy Greenfeld
7 x 10, 192 pp, illus., Quality PB, ISBN 1-58023-079-2 **$16.95**

Jewish Paths toward Healing and Wholeness: A Personal Guide to Dealing with Suffering *By Rabbi Kerry M. Olitzky. Foreword by Debbie Friedman.*
6 x 9, 192 pp, Quality PB, ISBN 1-58023-068-7 **$15.95**

Minding the Temple of the Soul
Balancing Body, Mind, and Spirit through Traditional Jewish Prayer, Movement, and Meditation *By Tamar Frankiel, Ph.D., and Judy Greenfeld*
7 x 10, 184 pp, illus., Quality PB, ISBN 1-879045-64-8 **$16.95**
Audiotape of the Blessings and Meditations: 60 min. **$9.95**
Videotape of the Movements and Meditations: 46 min. **$20.00**

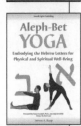

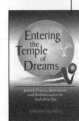

Spirituality/Women's Interest

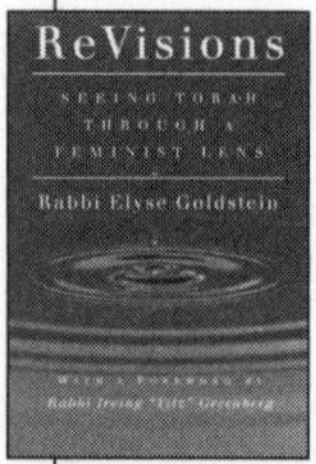

The Quotable Jewish Woman: Wisdom, Inspiration & Humor from the Mind & Heart *Edited and compiled by Elaine Bernstein Partnow*
The definitive collection of ideas, reflections, humor, and wit of over 300 Jewish women.
6 x 9, 496 pp, Hardcover, ISBN 1-58023-193-4 **$29.99**

Lifecycles, Vol. 1: Jewish Women on Life Passages & Personal Milestones
Edited and with introductions by Rabbi Debra Orenstein 6 x 9, 480 pp, Quality PB, ISBN 1-58023-018-0 **$19.95**

Lifecycles, Vol. 2: Jewish Women on Biblical Themes in Contemporary Life
Edited and with introductions by Rabbi Debra Orenstein and Rabbi Jane Rachel Litman
6 x 9, 464 pp, Quality PB, ISBN 1-58023-019-9 **$19.95**

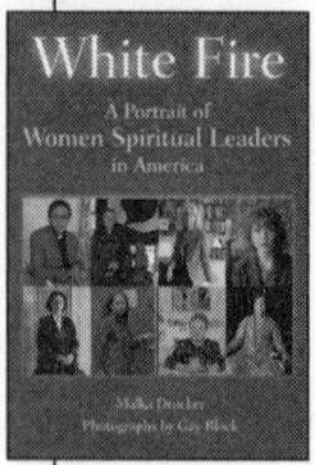

Moonbeams: A Hadassah Rosh Hodesh Guide *Edited by Carol Diament, Ph.D.*
8½ x 11, 240 pp, Quality PB, ISBN 1-58023-099-7 **$20.00**

ReVisions: Seeing Torah through a Feminist Lens *By Rabbi Elyse Goldstein*
5½ x 8½, 224 pp, Quality PB, ISBN 1-58023-117-9 **$16.95**

White Fire: A Portrait of Women Spiritual Leaders in America
By Rabbi Malka Drucker. Photographs by Gay Block.
7 x 10, 320 pp, 30+ b/w photos, Hardcover, ISBN 1-893361-64-0 **$24.95** *(A SkyLight Paths book)*

Women of the Wall: Claiming Sacred Ground at Judaism's Holy Site
Edited by Phyllis Chesler and Rivka Haut 6 x 9, 496 pp, b/w photos, Hardcover, ISBN 1-58023-161-6 **$34.95**

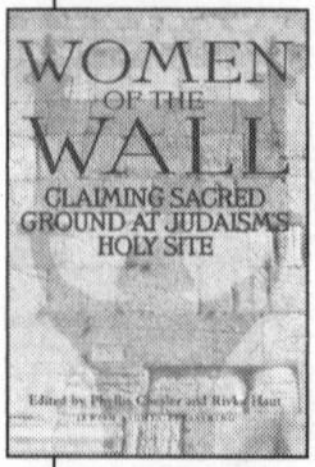

The Women's Haftarah Commentary: New Insights from Women Rabbis on the 54 Weekly Haftarah Portions, the 5 Megillot & Special Shabbatot
Edited by Rabbi Elyse Goldstein 6 x 9, 560 pp, Hardcover, ISBN 1-58023-133-0 **$39.99**

The Women's Torah Commentary: New Insights from Women Rabbis on the 54 Weekly Torah Portions *Edited by Rabbi Elyse Goldstein*
6 x 9, 496 pp, Hardcover, ISBN 1-58023-076-8 **$34.95**

The Year Mom Got Religion: One Woman's Midlife Journey into Judaism
By Lee Meyerhoff Hendler 6 x 9, 208 pp, Quality PB, ISBN 1-58023-070-9 **$15.95**

See Holidays for *The Women's Passover Companion: Women's Reflections on the Festival of Freedom* and *The Women's Seder Sourcebook: Rituals & Readings for Use at the Passover Seder.*

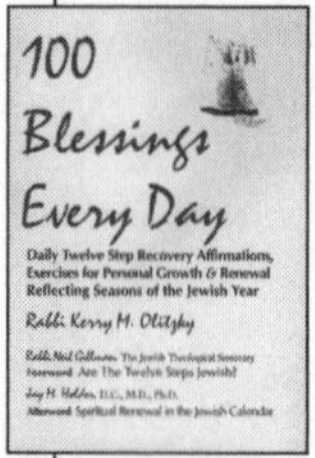

Travel

Israel—A Spiritual Travel Guide: A Companion for the Modern Jewish Pilgrim
By Rabbi Lawrence A. Hoffman 4¾ x 10, 256 pp, Quality PB, illus., ISBN 1-879045-56-7 **$18.95**
Also Available: **The Israel Mission Leader's Guide** ISBN 1-58023-085-7 **$4.95**

12 Steps

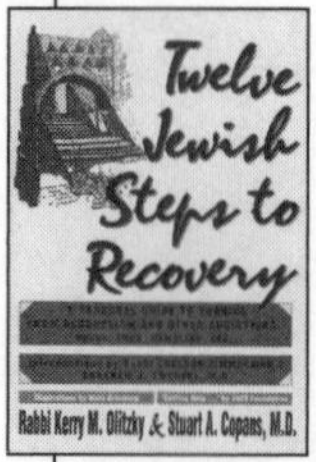

100 Blessings Every Day
Daily Twelve Step Recovery Affirmations, Exercises for Personal Growth & Renewal Reflecting Seasons of the Jewish Year
By Rabbi Kerry M. Olitzky. Foreword by Rabbi Neil Gillman.
One-day-at-a-time monthly format. Reflects on the rhythm of the Jewish calendar to bring insight to recovery from addictions.
4½ x 6½, 432 pp, Quality PB, ISBN 1-879045-30-3 **$15.99**

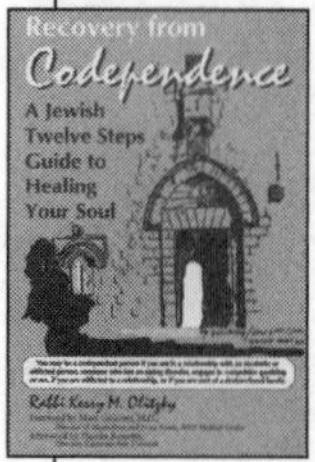

Recovery from Codependence: A Jewish Twelve Steps Guide to Healing Your Soul
By Rabbi Kerry M. Olitzky 6 x 9, 160 pp, Quality PB, ISBN 1-879045-32-X **$13.95**

Renewed Each Day: Daily Twelve Step Recovery Meditations Based on the Bible
By Rabbi Kerry M. Olitzky and Aaron Z.
Vol. 1—Genesis & Exodus: 6 x 9, 224 pp, Quality PB, ISBN 1-879045-12-5 **$14.95**
Vol. 2—Leviticus, Numbers & Deuteronomy: 6 x 9, 280 pp, Quality PB, ISBN 1-879045-13-3 **$14.95**

Twelve Jewish Steps to Recovery: A Personal Guide to Turning from Alcoholism & Other Addictions—Drugs, Food, Gambling, Sex...
By Rabbi Kerry M. Olitzky and Stuart A. Copans, M.D. Preface by Abraham J. Twerski, M.D.
6 x 9, 144 pp, Quality PB, ISBN 1-879045-09-5 **$14.95**